A Pocket Guide for Lightworkers
from
Archangel Metatron

...to meet future planetary chaos
and confusion within a peaceful
and harmonious perspective...

Ruth Anne Rhine

BALBOA
PRESS
A DIVISION OF HAY HOUSE

Balboa Press books may be ordered through booksellers or by contacting:

Balboa Press
A Division of Hay House
1663 Liberty Drive
Bloomington, IN 47403
www.balboapress.com
1 (877) 407-4847

Because of the dynamic nature of the Internet, any web addresses or links contained in this book may have changed since publication and may no longer be valid. The views expressed in this work are solely those of the author and do not necessarily reflect the views of the publisher, and the publisher hereby disclaims any responsibility for them.

The author of this book does not dispense medical advice or prescribe the use of any technique as a form of treatment for physical, emotional, or medical problems without the advice of a physician, either directly or indirectly. The intent of the author is only to offer information of a general nature to help you in your quest for emotional and spiritual well-being. In the event you use any of the information in this book for yourself, which is your constitutional right, the author and the publisher assume no responsibility for your actions.

The intent of this book is to share information to assist in the pursuit of growth spiritually, emotionally, and physically. Its author and publisher cannot take responsibility for how people may interpret and use the implied advice. Any suggestions utilized are for your own discernment.

Print information available on the last page.

ISBN: 978-1-9822-1535-4 (sc)
ISBN: 978-1-9822-1546-0 (e)

Library of Congress Control Number: 2018913020

Balboa Press rev. date: 10/31/2018

Dedicated to those who seek
the Kingdom of Heaven
upon the Earth

CONTENTS

PREFACE

FOR ALL DEAR HEARTS and Minds of those who seek the kingdom of heavenly healing and grace in ascending into the higher dimensional states of Being, do be advised to absorb the contents of this book for you shall attain the needed clarity and the needed assurance to traverse the years of turmoil and confusion ahead.

It is so, Dear Ones, that you succeed in ushering in the new paradigm now as you are the Light Beings who are to create Heaven upon the Earth without the worry and suffering for those who are conflicted still through the third dimensional experience in living. It is for you to disentangle from all dark influence and fear, and to send out loving light and healing to all the world everyday, free of the pain and suffering that plague your land and your hearts.

Do be advised to read the words lovingly channeled here as a gift from myself, Archangel Metatron, as I oversee your ascension process now and always. My channel is one of utmost devotion and service to the One of All That Is and so do not hesitate to trust in the words recorded here, for you are called to immerse your hearts and souls in the joy and the love that manifests now, and not something to wait upon in the future. You are the divine essence called to anchor the light of the Creator, and you are the ones who shall open the doors to many more to ascend through the heavenly gates of compassion and healing from all past sorrow and despair.

You are the Lightworkers who shall traverse with ease and joy the future unfoldment of Christed existence upon the earthly sphere of great and immense proportions. This small book is like a jewel in your pocket that you may reference any time, any day, when you feel the need for assurance and guidance so as to continue your journey in heart centered loving awareness, free of all fear and confusion. And so it is Dear Ones. And So It Is.

INTRODUCTION

Preparation for the Coming Changes

THERE IS A NEED for all those who read this book to reach into the furthest recesses of their soul and find within their being the strength and wisdom to remain centered throughout the coming year and coming decade for I, Archangel Metatron, shall assist you in endeavoring to awaken those who sleep yet amid the perils of the darkening landscape. Be not afraid nor disheartened, for this is only a process dawning upon humanity in order to purify and awaken the hearts of those who beckon grace and solace within their beings and So It Is.

This discourse is to be shared with those who wish to assist humanity in transitioning from an age of darkness into an age of light. You see, Dear Ones, this is naught for the hope of humankind, as it is for the presence of truth and love in being for all to experience within and without their troubled existence, for now is the time to release all manner of illusive thoughts and fears to open into the vast realities of Creator's Universe.

You need not be confused by external circumstances, nor by the appearance of darkening within the greater whole of humanity. This is a necessary process that the world is undergoing in order to experience awareness in new and wondrous existence, free of all dualistic, energetically conflictual arrangements in time and in space. See the light at the end of the tunnel, so to speak. See the Light within you and everyone now, and ignite the love in everyone's heart through kindness and presence of Christed loving acceptance of all things as they currently exist.

Do not fear. I repeat, do not fear for I, Archangel Metatron, am with you every step, and your protection and support are insured as you carry greater and greater amounts of light within your being so as to uplift the hearts of those who live in darkness. This is not to say that you entangle or sacrifice your well being to any degree. This is to say, simply be the presence of trust and faith in Creator's Grace that all is well my friends. All Is Well.

It is my wish for all Lightworkers to not be confused by any turn of events that distort the truth and love of the Creator, and remain steadfast in their lightwork upon this planet. They are greatly needed in order to assist those who wish to be free in dissolving all illusion and distrust due to needless worry and concern over that which they do not understand.

Now is the time to seek resolution for it is now upon us all to endeavor to greater and greater heights of awareness, so as to reveal the truth of our beings to ourselves, one another, and to the greater mass population. By this I mean we endeavor to emanate the love we embody out to everyone we encounter, to everyone we meet, to all who exist within our sphere of existence, so as to activate the heart centers of those who are lost in the depths of their despair and sorrow and have yet to awaken. This means we choose to become conscious in every moment of our divine purpose in being.

Dear Ones, time is not to waste, for now we are upon the precipice of a new paradigm, and so we must prepare ourselves to relinquish all that would hold us back in giving freely of our love to all humanity and to all who exist upon this planet. We are not to fear and are not to doubt our own cognitive experience of our inner truth as manifest upon this planet. And so to not allow being swayed by the current regime of political and environmental devastation, as it is simply a process the Earth is undergoing so as to embroil the karmic repercussions that exist throughout all timelines converging at this point in your lives.

You see, Dear Ones, the premise pronounced at the time of your current incarnation's birth has now come full circle into fruition of your life's purpose. And you may exalt and take great joy in the knowing that you have arrived at the right place and the right time, so as to enable your work in uplifting humanity to reach fulfillment in new ways never before experienced. Now we see upon the horizon the promise of great awakening within the hearts and minds of those who sleep, and it is your love, your light, which is the key to unlocking their conscious awareness of evolutionary growth. Be not afraid. Be not afraid to reveal your truth as you see it, for it shall be received with great appreciation and receptivity by those who seek this truth within themselves and So It Is.

1

The Time Is Now

NOW IS THE TIME to understand that all of nature and the cycles of Mother Earth are effectual in maintaining balance for the planetary survival and evolution of all who exist upon her. For she is a powerful and loving being, who having made great sacrifice for her children, has now declared that her ascension process be for not only her own well-being, but also for those who wish to be released from this energetic entanglement and elevated into the higher frequencies of Light and Love.

This is not to say that all beings have made this choice on a soul level, as some beings wish to experience more of the dualistic behaviors existing here now and will, without judgment, be allowed to continue their journey for further experiencing of this particular dimensional plane. There are those whose evolutionary path are not yet complete in their development so as to allow them to ascend with the Earth, however, they will indeed ascend at some point as they are all within Creator's loving embrace and shall eventually ascend at a time when they are fulfilled with their experience of dualistic existence.

Now is the time for all Lightworkers to seek solace within community with those of like mind, so as to feel supported and able to exercise the loving relationships of the new paradigm now in their current existence. The time is now to move forward with all visions of higher expression of your soul embodied manifestation of the great I AM presence within the One of All That Is, and this is happening to those who choose to evolve naturally within the ascension cycles of Mother Earth. It is as though you are all easily and naturally unfolding into the beautiful flowers you are without need of resistance and fear holding you back on any level of your being.

And I, Archangel Metatron, shall release your angst and fear within your entire being should you wish this to be so. Simply ask for my assistance and I shall respond in ways you may not comprehend, however, you shall continue to heal and unfold in the grace of the love of who you truly are. Blessings to You upon this day and everyday. I, Archangel Metatron, shall reside within the hearts and minds of those who comprehend these words and So It Is.

2

Freedom From Within

FOR IT IS KNOWN in the Heavens and upon the Earth that the tides of change are upon us, and we seek to be free of the discord surrounding us borne of the dark influence on all of humanity. Do we wish to continue our existence within the parameters of dualistic behaviors, or shall we move into the new paradigm of harmonious resonance within the peace and joy and love in living our truth? You see, my Dear Ones, now we embark upon a journey into the soul of our own beings and I, Archangel Metatron, shall guide and direct your attention throughout so as to keep steady your focus and peaceful your mind. It is now time to have all hearts and minds harmoniously expressed through our intent to ascend into the Divinity of Who We Truly Are, and this time is upon us.

After much preparation we can be assured that we are ready to endure the coming changes upon the Earth, while holding fast to the love and compassion within our hearts and beings. We have more to endure of the effects of the dark; however, it need not affect us personally, for we are beings of divine inspiration, and we seek to live in the flow of Creator's light and love. Holding to this center of peaceful reliance and bold courageous movement will carry us through to brighter days of existence, all the while assisting and aiding those in need of our help, so that they may move into alignment with the energetic flow of the Earth's Ascension Process and So It Is

3

Need for Understanding

DEAR ONES, TODAY I SPEAK to you of more and more love entering through your hearts, minds, and souls, for you are vehicles of light and wonder, manifesting miracle upon miracle here upon the Earth. You see there are no limits to your ability to heal and create joy upon this planet, and so do not feel you are incapable of making this world, not only better, but also a divine expression of Creator's Being. The time to separate yourself from others is over, for now you see the unity of all things and also the interconnectedness of all manifest realities, and so for you to seek solace with like minded others is beneficial for all. As in groups, you become exponentially more powerful in creating an impact upon the world and all sentient beings existing here.

Do not be alarmed at the vehicles of media outlets, and also any fear mongering put forth by your governmental control systems, for they do not hold the transformative power that exists within your hearts. Dear Ones, be not afraid. Be not afraid. Be not afraid on any level of your being, for the darkness that exists is illusion and cannot harm you when you perceive your life with loving intent and action. There are no possible means to eradicate the light through dark intent and dark action, for you see only light can extinguish the dark. The dark can never extinguish the Light and So It Is.

Now dawning upon this planet are the avenues available for new life and living in resonance with divine flow of Creator's Essence. And so live your lives in the new paradigm now, without fear or concern as to what actions are taken by those who have obscured their light though illusive existence. Finding truth in all things is finding the truth within your own being as everything is manifest of the One Divine Essence. Being one with your own being is to be One with All That Is. And so when you experience discord in the world, and within your own selves, take a deep breath, Dear Ones, and know that this discord is simply an expression of interference of your divine alignment with your truth. And so, yes, take a breath and realign your heart and mind with the beauty within your soul and So It Is.

4

The Trumpet Calls

NOW WE SEE upon the horizon new means to implement our loving service to humanity and all beings upon the Earth. Dear Ones, do hear the trumpet call your hearts and minds together, for now all must devote to their divine purpose in being, and that is to extinguish all darkness within your dimensional plane of being. We seek to eradicate all doubt and fear and all illusive beliefs that prevent the presence of Divinity within our Beings.

You have the capacity to override all collective, mindful interference that would interrupt divine inspiration and flow of Creator's manifest action and deeds of loving intent. Do be aware that we are not alone and are in the company of Great Beings from other star systems who are present for the purpose to empower and bless your healing work through the multifaceted means through which you emanate your love and creativity. Do be aware of more than simply loving intent. Be aware of immense assistance that supports your intent, as this is due to the connectivity of the One of All That Is manifest through multitudinous Light Beings surrounding your planet.

Now we see upon the horizon the Unity of All Beings, not only within your planet, but also your entire star system, your entire Universe, as well as the Multiverse, for we are One now and eternally. And so take great joy in this knowing and being of the Collective Universal Consciousness of One Heart and One Mind. In this knowing we reside in peace, and love, and fulfillment of our heart's alignment with Truth and So It Is.

5

Always In All Ways

THERE IS UPON US a time of reckoning that presents new challenges into our existence. The developmental times upon us are vast and deep in that we are continuing our process of evolutionary development, while at the same time, we are also extending our own beings in service to assist the planet, and also other beings in need of assistance to ascend into the divinity of who we truly are: the Light and Love of Creator's Essence.

Now we see many opportunities to grow in new directions and also within unlimited avenues of promise and joy, in that we continue to release what no longer serves our well being and soul. And so I, Archangel Metatron, shall assist those who wish, to release more angst and grief carried in the heart and soul that inhibit the flow of Creator's Divine Light.

You see, Dear Ones, there are no limits upon your ability to bestow powerful manifestations of joy and love upon your own beings and the beings you encounter in your existence, for you are indeed the essence and truth of that which you are.

Now, Dear Ones, trust that you shall receive all that you desire to empower your development for your soul expression into your outer existence, for the inner truth is one and the same as the outer. As you clear and become vessels of divine flow, you will find your lives becoming easier and more manageable without the stress of ordinary living. You shall succeed in your heartfelt endeavors without angst or worry, for you have the love and support of your inner truth becoming manifest in your outward reality.

Know this. Be this. Live this. And It Is So.

6

All Is Well

TODAY I SHALL INSTRUCT YOU, Dear Ones, as to how to succeed in your healing work without need of worry or concern as to how your intentions are implemented, for I, Archangel Metatron, oversee the vast majority of Lightworkers who intend to uplift and heal the planet and all beings upon her manifest Soul. We find ourselves at an impasse that beckons greater awareness and love that may sometimes feel encumbering to you. However, do not be burdened by the woes of the world for all is well within the inner and outer planes of existence, for I can see throughout all timelines, and what I see is a beautiful unfoldment of grace and healing showering your sphere of being and So It Is.

Now you seek to know greater and greater amounts of undeniable proof that indeed all is well, for you wish to see the results of your work manifest within the outer plans due to your need to feel gratified for your work and loving intent. It is not for you to judge the outer appearance of the world, for the world does not reveal the internal workings of the effects of Grace as you might like. You see, Dear Ones, the process of Divine Grace and Intervention is a process that happens within the hearts and minds and souls of all those who are open to this energetic healing and cleansing of spiritual obstructions and hindering beliefs. All do not wish to ascend at this time, and so free will choice comes into play, and some choose to remain within the outer dimensional expression of being within the limitations of dualistic experience.

We seek to know that all is well and not just words we hear. Look into your hearts, Dear Ones, and see the truth of your own being evolving and growing in wondrous ways, and then you shall know within your own self that all is well. To accept the world's unfoldment of chaos as not entirely a reflection of you personally, but a reflection of the collective mind upon your planet, you may be assured that although chaos ensues upon the Earth, you, Dear Ones, and those who seek the Kingdom of Truth within, shall manifest your internal experience outwardly into your external reality, and this transpires through the intent of your heart's loving presence.

It is not to say that there are not challenges ahead for each of you; however, when you embark upon a healing and enlightening process, you shall receive the grace necessary to ascend into the Light of your Beings and Souls. Now, to become more and more of the love and light that you truly are I, Archangel Metatron, suggest you call upon me for guidance and healing, and so I shall respond in loving implementation of your heartfelt request, and So It Is.

There are those of you who may doubt the unfoldment of the ascension process; however, there is no need for your confusion when you listen to the rhythmic pulsation emanating from within your planetary sphere of divine presence. Allow this soothing pulsation assure you All Is Well.

7

The Knowing Heart

THERE ARE MORE ENERGIES in play within your beings and souls than you can imagine for Divine Grace showers upon and through your Beings. Becoming aware of the mighty love and healing power you do embody is important to be aware of so that you can manifest and emanate this immense power and grace out into your realm of existence. For you see, there are no limits upon the amount of love you can express. Love is infinite in its nature as it is the Body and Soul of the Creator itself. Love is the grace and the power and the light which guides and directs your heartfelt purpose.

When you feel at a loss for what to do or what to say or where to go, simply go into your heart of hearts, and allow the divine essence of love to flow. Connecting into it will fulfill your needs required at the moment. Trust your own Heart and So It Is. Now you see before you immense opportunity to grow and expand, and this opportunity is available for everyone who wishes to ascend with your beautiful Mother Earth. She supports your development as well as your well being, so that you can thrive and ascend into greater and greater heights of consciousness.

You see there are many ways in which you can assist in healing your planet, and each of you have specific talents to express this. And so to follow your intuitive perception in your life's direction is to connect into your individual soul expression unique to your ability to perceive what means are called for to heal a particular situation, person, plant, animal, element, and any and all sentient life upon and within the Earth. Do know that you may always call upon me, Archangel Metatron, for I can assist you in many ways and means throughout your Dimensional Being and So It Is.

8

The Purpose of Ascension

FOR WE SEE NOW it is a time to contemplate the meaning of what Ascension truly is. Ascension is like a transport system that enables us to arise into greater and greater awareness within our hearts, our minds, our bodies, and our soul. For there is only Truth, and the light of that truth is manifest in all things living within and without our existence upon the Earth and within the inner planes of Creator's manifest Universe.

We come to our ascended state through the clearing and letting go of all dualistic behaviors and beliefs, so that we may encapsulate higher dimensional awareness of the integral nature of existence, for there is no separation between the inner and outer plans of consciousness. What is known within us manifests externally in the world around us. There are many avenues for this process, as many avenues as there are stars in the sky and grains of sand upon the shores.

Do not hesitate to call upon me, Archangel Metatron, for I am present within your hearts and minds and will respond to your beckon call through the Oneness of All That Is. Please remember to ask what you wish assistance with, and I shall respond accordingly for your highest and best good.

Ascension is meant to be a passage way between dimensional interrelated fields of conscious expansion into greater soul presence. What can obscure and hinder this natural state of expansion are the dualistic belief systems that have been present upon the Earth for many eons of time, and so the influence of dark energetic control prevents this natural process. Therefore, I, Archangel Metatron, shall assist all those who wish to be elevated into higher dimension upliftment so that you may understand the true nature of your being.

Now we see that there are still obstructions for many, and so it is time to focus upon healing and clearing yourselves, and others who seek your assistance in healing their illusive stance in being. Do not be concerned that this process of Ascension will not manifest for you, as all that is required is openness and willingness to move forward in letting go of all that hinders your development. Ascension will reveal your innate remembrance of your inner truth, and then you shall glide my friends. You shall glide with ease into higher dimensions of Being, while at the same time embodying your earthly presence.

This is the beautiful thing about Ascension. You may reside upon the Earth and also be consciously present within dimensional awareness in Being. The connectivity you experience with all manifest upon the Earth and the Universe, shall fulfill your every need as your journey unfolds in the trust you hold and in the love you emanate and So It Is.

9

Opening of Hearts

AND AS THE NEW DAY DAWNS upon us, we see in the distance avenues opening within our hearts and minds that lead to greater awareness and understanding of the process of Ascension. It unfolds with such ease and beauty as never before revealed to those upon the Earth plane while still physically manifest. This is a long awaited gift for you, who have sought fearlessly and faithfully, all manner of being to pursue the path of love and light.

Never again to doubt the reality of divine presence within your heart and soul, you shall experience multitudinous facets of loving relationship with Creator's benevolent expression in Being. Pleased to be, and pleased to act as an instrument of God's Grace and Light now and forever more, you shall expand and grow beyond your wildest imaginings, as it is not possible to fathom the depths and heights of Creator's vast and powerful presence throughout the world, the Universe, and so far beyond the infinite nature of the Multiverse.

Know this, Dear Ones, for you are to be in the forefront of those ascending now so as to light the way for others. You have broken ground, so to speak, and it is for you to realize the importance of your work for your own selves and for those whom you lead and assist. Your impact upon the world is immeasurable and I, Archangel Metatron, Bless You in ways you cannot possibly imagine. I Love You unconditionally and accept the process of your growth without question, as I know and see that your paths all lead into the Heart of the One of All That Is. Blessings of joy shower now upon you to fortify and strengthen your resolve in continuing your devotion in service to all. And So It Is.

10

May Peace Reside Within You

PEACE BE WITH YOU in the days ahead for there are times of turmoil before you, and so I, Archangel Metatron, say to you, do not be afraid or disempowered, for there will be resolution and rectification in time. It is not for you to fully understand the course of future events, or even to be concerned that the dire repercussions of wrongful thoughts and wrongful actions shall be of a problematic nature for you, as you are allowed to make mistakes and misunderstand the turn of events.

For there will be for you, many days and many ways to survive amid the chaos, while at the same time be in good cheer and of great service to those who seek your help in progressing through the Ascension process. All the while, many shall follow avenues of dualistic experience through their choosing, and this is not for you to judge, as there are multitudinous pathways that shall eventually all lead into the Heart of the Creator in each one's own time and experience.

Be at peace, Dear Ones, for we are now at an impasse of inevitable future events that forebode much chaos and confusion. Do not be concerned that some appear to suffer more than others. For each individual may choose their own path of experience in this realm of being, and it is not for us to say nor to understand the true nature of an individual's choice in the elevation of their growth in being.

For now we see, Dear Ones, various outlets for growth and healing to allow many more beings to ascend than believed possible ever before. We seek to assist as many beings as can be, so that more and more beloved Lightworkers may be put to the test to attain higher and higher amounts of healing energetic transmissions to transmit into, and throughout the Earth plane to all who can receive these gifts of uplifting grace. Do not hesitate to call upon me, Archangel Metatron, so that I may assist you in whatever way you should require in order to continue to heal and clear, and absorb divine light, so as to expand and become the Truth of Who You Are.

Be at peace, Dear Ones, for now we see that All Is Well for One and All, as the capitulation of those who seek loving existence shall reap the rewards of many lifetimes of service and devotion. There is no right or wrong in action truly, only action aligned with the Creator's intent to exist in harmonious resonance in being. You can make no mistakes, only continue to learn to balance and align your being within your own heart and soul. Be at peace in the knowing that All Is Well and So It Is.

11

Never Before Upon The Earth

NEVER HAS IT BEEN SAID, nor has it been enacted upon the human race, that prior lifetimes of experience are now being cleared and healed so that those who wish to ascend may do so without the need to be obstructed by karmic blocks to Ascension and So It Is. My friends, do know that there are some lessons that do require completion; however, it is no longer necessary to suffer dualistic reactivity here upon the Earth. Your time of suffering is at an end. It is for you to know that there are forces at work that allow you to seek solace within the wisdom of your hearts, so that you are in a constant state of joy and love, without the fears and trepidations that formerly plagued your existence.

Although there still exists chaos and dramatic events affecting the many who still choose this dualistic experience, for those who seek to live in alignment with Creator's Grace this is not so. For the Lightworkers and those who are meeting the challenges presented to them in order to grow and uplift their conscious awareness, there are no longer choices to be made as they have sealed their devotion and sense of service to making this world not just better, but perfectly aligned with the love and light of Creator's Divine Presence.

Know this, Dear Ones. Know that there are numerous avenues of loving grace and forgiveness available to you all who wish this transitional experience of evolutionary growth into the higher realms of Being connecting into the Oneness of All That Is. Dear Ones, the benevolent nature of your life's journey is structured so that you may have more time to serve your divine purpose in being. Which is to say you are being allowed to find pathways never open before that allow you to exist without strain and stress, so that you can relax and live in perpetual flow of the support and protection and abundance of the Creator.

Now and again I, Archangel Metatron, say to you, be at peace Dear Ones. Be at peace, for no longer are you required to struggle or suffer, only to continue the ever evolving journey into the Heart of the Creator. Be at peace in the knowing, and the expression of love and joy and abundant flow of divine grace within and without your Being and So It Is.

12

No Matter Great or Small

FOR NOW IT IS KNOWN in the Heavens and upon the Earth that all beings, great and small, shall have a day of reckoning that will reveal their chosen intent to ascend and continue their journey into the vastness of their own Being, for there is no limit nor end to our evolutionary growth. We are the Starseeds that cultivate beauty and healthful expressions of Creator's Divine Grace here upon the inner and outer planes of existence and so I say to You, you shall reap the grand and noble and amazing benefits of living in divine presence now and forever more.

Dear Ones, do not be alarmed when the trumpet calls for you to ascend, for you shall awaken to remembrance of your inner truth and presence that has never left you, has never been separate from you, only sleeping within your subconscious mind. There are great and wondrous abilities and talents that will manifest throughout your being and soul. And so do not fear a loss of identity, for you shall now only awaken to your true identity. All the while it has been within you in a dormant state.

For you see, Dear Ones, life is an ever present movement of Creator's loving expression in perpetual motion, as all life goes in cyclic development of evolutionary growth within the souls of every being, great and small. There is no separation in this, as all beings upon the Earth are of

One Essence and of One Mind and of One Heart. And so I say to you, Dear Ones, do not cry or feel remorseful for those who are still evolving through the expressions of dualistic behavior, for they are indeed within their own process which is just as essential to their growth as your process now is to yours.

You see all is well in this way, for each being, no matter great or small, is indeed exactly experiencing what they require to eventually ascend into their greater awareness of who they are, for all suffering is illusion. As beneath the dramatic outplays of grief and sorrow is the divine presence of who they truly are, and when they emerge into the wholeness of their being, just as you are now, they shall also experience their day of reckoning in their own time, and in their own way. It is not for us to judge the chosen paths of those who appear to be left behind, for they are not. They are simply taking the route to self awareness through choices made that best benefit their soul and soul growth. So do not be in dismay that all does not feel right in the world, as all is well in actuality, Dear Ones. All Is Well.

Never doubt the truth of who you are and never doubt the expression of Creator's plan for all to ascend in their own way, in their own time. Now, there is indeed a sense of wonder as to how this is so, when the world does not seem to be in a harmonious state, but one of corruption and confusion. And so I say Dear Ones, although the outward imagery surrounding you is paradoxical in that it appears that chaos reigns globally, it is not. For all manifestations of Creator are perfect expressions of their free will choices as to how they wish to evolve into alignment with divine flow and So It Is.

13

Always Know the Truth of Your Own Heart

AND NOW WE BEGIN TO SEE the results of our efforts to heal and ascend, as we open our hearts and minds to greater amounts of light, to benefit not only ourselves, but also those we encounter who have the openness to receive our light emanating from within. Always know that you may encounter those who are not able to receive your love for they are traveling a different course than the one you have embarked upon. So do not feel inadequate in your work, for it is of no matter as to whether or not another being receives Creator's grace at this particular juncture.

You see, Dear Ones, now there is more for you to understand regarding the nature of the dualistic experience you exist within. You have more options as to how to heal and remove all limiting beliefs and obscurations that create and separate you from the truth of the One of All That Is. Forever more you are free of the suffering that has separated you through illusive avenues of dualistic reactive behaviors, as you choose to respond through your knowing heart to the challenges that may present themselves still in your lives.

Always know that I, Archangel Metatron, shall be present with you in assisting your ability to withstand and overcome all obstacles you encounter now and in the future, as you move through greater and greater fields of awareness of who you truly are. Always know you are with the Angels of Ascension who shall provide all that you require, to not only survive the coming days of havoc and turmoil, but also all you require to exist in peace, joy, and harmonious union with likeminded others who share in community of mutual support of the ascension process all are experiencing together. Now is the time to seek out those you resonate with through your intent to connect more clearly with those who are also in the process of ascension, so that you may join others who understand and support your evolutionary development.

Always know that I, Archangel Metatron, shall be by your side should you ever feel confused by external events that appear traumatic to those who experience them. I shall bring clarity within your hearts and minds so that you do not become entangled in the suffering that no longer envelops your existence. Your loving compassion shall arise and give way to a more appropriate response rather than to experience the suffering of those who are choosing their own experience. Know that you may call upon me, Archangel Metatron, for guidance and support so that you can remain in the divine flow of Creator's Grace.

It is not unkind or uncaring to no longer feel the suffering of others when you actually do care that they find healing and happiness in their lives. You simply accept that they choose to experience struggle and karmic repercussions in order to learn and grow and evolve, just as you have through your own karmic experiences. Sending them love and light shall assist them greatly without the need to feel their suffering your own selves. It is of no value to feel their pain. It is of value, however, to express your love for those who still suffer and So It Is.

14

Now It Is Known Upon the Earth

I WISH TO TELL YOU all that now more than ever, it is required to become a greater influence upon those around you whom you encounter, for your presence and your actions will allow them to open to greater amounts of love within themselves. I wish to say to you that you have the ability to transform and to transmute energetic blocks and hindrances within not only yourselves, but also others, and do not doubt that through your intentions this can be so simply by wishing this to take place.

For example, when you are present with another whom you feel is resistant to their soul embodiment of love, you may simply send them love from your heart intending that it dissolve their resistance to loving themselves and others. Needing to see the best within those whom you encounter is important, for they then can experience their own higher nature, as there are numerous means and ways that a being may awaken to their own Truth. Do not underestimate the importance of your ability to reflect these attributes, to reveal to them the light they also hold.

So be it known on Earth and in the Heavens that All Is Well and that all is unfolding in perfect grace through the expression of Creator's Divine Presence within and without your dimensional experience. For now it is known by the many, who are open to the healing grace bestowed upon the masses upon your planet, that there are numerous means to move into the higher dimensions of Being through magnificent and magical energetic assistance from Higher Dimensional Beings of Light within the inner and outer planes.

Do not hesitate to call upon me, Archangel Metatron, for guidance and assistance in clearing the way for your Ascension and evolution in becoming greater and greater reservoirs of loving light. It is now known that peace and harmonious flow reside within the hearts of those who are conscious of their soul connection to All That Is. Enjoy the knowledge of this and merge ever more deeply into the Heart of the One and So It Is.

15

There Is No Need to Fear

PEACE BE WITH YOU, Dear Ones, on this day of evolutionary growth residing within your hearts and minds, for it is known upon the Earth and in the Heavens that All Is Well. In reading thus far, you are aware of what has been delivered before that leads you to this page of continued support and enlightened information as to how to co-exist with the planetary turmoil, without becoming entangled in the influences of chaos and fear.

Now before us, is a path carved through the heartfelt longing for peace in the world and also the desire to live in harmonious flow of Creator's Divine Presence. I say to you, Dear Ones, I, Archangel Metatron, shall oversee your process of Ascension so as to insure you shall be safe and be of good cheer during the tumultuous days ahead, when confusion and discord reign upon the Earth. I wish not to be a naysayer; I only wish to prepare you for probable outcomes that could alarm you. Be not afraid for All Is Well. I cannot emphasize this enough so that you integrate this understanding into your daily existence.

I, Archangel Metatron, shall uplift the hearts and minds of all who wish to ascend through the dimensional portals of Divine Grace in order to elevate your being into the embodiment of your own inner Truth and So It Is. Now is the moment you have prepared for, and now is the time to reach out into your communities to offer your healing and guidance to those who are open to receiving your Light and Wisdom. Do not fear exposing yourselves to the general public in this way, as your ascension course shall lead you in the right direction, insuring that you shall always reside and move along divinely orchestrated avenues of expression.

There is no need to withhold or to hide your talents and gifts any longer for fear of scrutiny or judgment. For those who receive shall know your sincere intent to assist them, and they will be grateful and acknowledge your efforts through their receptive nature. Any being who does not choose to ascend shall not be drawn to your sphere of existence, and you will not need to be concerned about indifference to your work.

Now is the time to move forward without hesitation in revealing the nature of your work for many are waiting for your help. Go forward with confidence and know that your light is shining into the hearts of those around you. In the times ahead, be focused upon your ability to lovingly reach out to others so that we may awaken more and more beings to their own light and truth. Love is the answer to every challenge, every problem, every imbalance, that manifests within your lives and in the lives of others. And so go forth, Dear Ones, in complete confidence that your are cradled in the loving embrace of God's protection and support. Fear Not, for All Is Well.

16

Be It Known That Heaven Above Shall Exist Upon Earth in Due Time

FOREMOST AND ABOVE ALL I, Archangel Metatron, shall assist in all things that may dissuade you from moving forward upon your ascension path. For there is nothing that can actually prevent you from ascending at this time, when all avenues into the Divine Presence of Being are open to you, and everyone who wishes to embody their divine truth. Be it known on Earth that the intentions of healing the planet and all inhabitants shall ring true in the coming decades. For now, suffice it to say, the process you are all undergoing is promising peace and joy upon the horizon before you. Trust and It Is So.

Dear Ones, love is enveloping the Earth, and the world surrounding you is filled with the grace of Creator's Divinity. And so be not afraid to step into the world with confidence, for your pathway is lit in golden light, and you simply need follow this 'yellow brick road' so to speak. Your days upon the Earth are blessed with genuine knowing of this promise, and all you need do is accept the gifts of grace that manifest before you, as you journey throughout your timeline upon the hills and valleys of your existence.

Always keep in mind that thunderous events shall occur now and in the future; however, you have the power and the ability to withstand all chaos due to your knowing that all is well. Never before has there been such love and grace bestowed upon the beings of Earth, as many are at an impasse to which they may choose to ascend. And for those who have and will, there is all manner of assistance pouring into their hearts and minds to allow them to progress with ease, and loving assurance that their ascension process will unfold perfectly.

Fear Not for All Is Well.

Fear Not for All Is Well.

Fear Not for All Is Well.

Prior to today's discourse there has been much discussion of what this involves in the knowing that 'All Is Well' and so you may wish to start at the beginning of this books discourse to catch up to where we are now, so that the following will be better understood.

Dear Ones, your love is powerful beyond your knowing, and you may move mountains indeed, through your loving intentions and prayers to heal the Earth, and one another. Be it said that at this moment many more beings are opening to receive the grace and love you embody, and so do not feel discouraged at the dismal events that will transpire, as they are not of your making and also not of your choosing. It is possible for all beings here on Earth to travel their own distinct path coinciding with your existence, and will not in anyway alter your 'path of gold' to greater and greater heights of loving presence of Creator's Divine Grace. Know this is so, and It Is So.

17

Always in the Heart

ALWAYS THERE IS MEANING to what is said when the heart is open, for there truth lies, and is expressed either energetically through thought, word, and deed, and yes, Dear Ones, through your intentions to do good in the world overall. For the heart is an organ that allows you to live through moving liquid light and nutrients throughout your physical and energetic being, and is also the prime conduit for your soul expression in being. There is no separation in this. There is only the unity and the expression of the love innate within every heart in existence.

It is only when the heart is obscured by fear and doubt that this expression is hindered, and so know that in the course of events now unfolding I, Archangel Metatron, shall assist you in releasing what hinders your heart's pure expression of love. All that you need do is ask, for in the flow of Ascension, it is not necessary for you to understand all that transpires in the course of healing your heart, mind, body, and soul.

Be it known on this day, that all those who have chosen to ascend, shall receive the grace of Creator's love and healing within and without your fields of expression, so that you may emanate your true self unhindered any longer by fear and false beliefs that limit your ability to expand and grow. Now it is known by all who wish to receive Creator's Divine Presence within their being that they will, and of certainty attain the liberation they seek for themselves, and also enable many others to do the same, and So It Is. Peace reigns in the hearts of those who seek the Kingdom of Love within.

18

You Have Great Power to Change the World

NOW WE SHALL BEGIN a new process of healing the planet and those upon it, so that the dark influences currently raging throughout the globe are dissolved and uplifted. And so I ask of the Lightworkers to take a moment each day to send the love and light from their hearts into the Earth and out to all who inhabit her, regardless of what form is manifest. It is simply achieved through intent to heal and clear all dark discordant energies, through the hearts of Creator's Love within every Being and So It Is.

You may feel this is a small thing, and I, Archangel Metatron, assure you it is not. For when you open your heart to allow the light of the Creator to pour forth into the world, it is magical in that this energy can transform and uplift the hearts of many, without having to make a public proclamation of this intent. It is like a silent prayer for peace and love for everyone and everything. Just a moment spent with this intent can move mountains when many join in purpose unifying intent to exist in harmonious presence now and forever more.

Dear Ones, it is not enough to simply think that all is well when the Earth can benefit so much more from your active participation in the healing process. It is beneficial for all Lightworkers to join in purpose to accelerate the healing of this planet, as this does, and will make a tremendous difference to the healing process everyone and everything is now currently experiencing. It is not to be that All Is Well simply because in time it is known to be. It is greatly enhanced through the co-creative process of all Beings who consciously take responsibility for channeling their many gifts and healing love out into the world.

Dear Ones, your grace and loving intent shall make the difference for many more beings on Earth to ascend. And know this is so, because you are uplifting and supporting and holding space for those who are lost, so that they may find their way into the Truth of their own Hearts and So It Is.

19

Knowing Is Not to Judge

RECTIFICATION OF BEING always in the right is due to the need to align with one's own truth. However, this is not to say that what is right for one, is what is right for another. For in being aligned, while still clinging to the idea that this is the only truth, creates judgment of oneself and others resulting in the illusion of separation. A Lightworker may unknowingly feel superior to others who have not awakened, due to their strong desire to exist within the truth of their being, while viewing others as inferior who do not seek this awareness.

And so I say to you, Dear Ones, do not become entangled in the expression of elevating yourselves through this form of comparison. It contributes to separation from others, and hinders the ability to clearly see in responding to them, while withholding judgment of any form for any reason regardless of how another appears. Always allow and hold space for them to exist in their own process, although it may not align with yours. Lightworkers evolve, and heal themselves and others, through the knowing of their own cognizance of being One With All That Is. To conceive themselves as separate from others due to their evolved state of being is not only illusive but also not in the spirit of giving freely from their knowing hearts.

I cannot emphasize this idea enough so that all Lightworkers exist in a state of humble and honorable knowing that they are integral to the unfoldment of Earth's ascension process, for they are simply manifesting their abilities through their awareness that All Is One. You see, Dear Ones, it is not for you to judge your own self worth, anymore than the worth of others, for ALL are upon a path of greater awakening and awareness through whatever means they have chosen. And so do not elevate your importance over anyone or anything as this contributes to the illusion of separation.

Dear Ones, I do value greatly who you are, and what you accomplish, which is to say that you are Divine Beings of Light in service to humanity. I simply ask that you remain in a humble stance in relation to others you encounter, so that there is openness in perception of seeing with clarity and love the truth within All beings. For it is true that some will not respond or understand your work; however, this is not to say that they are 'lost souls' for they are not. They are simply in a different stance of reality, in view of what they need to experience in order to grow into the truth of their own being, and this is not to be judged. For in judging others we judge ourselves, which creates and solidifies the belief that we are separate and we are not.

Dear Ones, this is not to say, that you are not evolved beyond the ordinary existence of your planetary reality. It is to say, that although you are ascending while some may not at this juncture, it is still important and perfect that everyone continues their evolutionary journey with the respect and acceptance that All Is Well for One and All and So It Is.

20

Be Not Afraid To Love Fully
Love With Open Heart

TODAY IS ANOTHER DAY where we shall explore the stance of Lightworkers across the globe who devote themselves to healing the Earth and those who reside here. For you are aware that the entirety of who you are encompasses also the entire Universe, as well as the Multiverse and beyond. Be not afraid to embrace the Heart and Soul of Mother Earth, for she is you and you are she and So It Is.

Dear Ones, be not afraid to extend your hearts to embrace everyone and everything, for this is the calling of your own truth and divine essence. Please always understand that in being, you are the divine love of the Creator, and so it is throughout all existence. Be not afraid to expand your horizons to embody greater and greater amounts of light and love, and to connect into the reality of your divinity, letting go of preconceived notions that you are finite, due to earthly indoctrinations of behavior within this dimensional perspective. Know that your heart and mind manifest from deep within your being to express great love, when unencumbered by thoughts and beliefs that hinder your clarity.

It is for you to perceive that there are numerous expressions of loving grace that you can merge and synthesize with, in order to expand your godly perspective of All That Is, from the view point of your Divine Self, rather than only your earthly perspective. Know that your ability to embrace more and more love is a natural process in your evolution of greater soul embodiment. It is effortless, requiring only the letting go of emotional and mental entanglement of the earthly perspective of dualistic behavior, and this is achieved through your intention to do so, and allow Divine Grace to assist you daily in asking for this to be so.

You shall find that avenues of healing and clearing open wide for you to achieve your heart's desire to become a clear vessel of light and love. Never doubt this to be untrue, for you shall always have the blessing of the Creator, and you shall always have the support of the Creator in being and realizing your inner truth, and this shall manifest as your outer truth as well as there is no separation in this.

21

When Tragedy Erupts

TRAGIC EVENTS COMPEL ME to speak of traumatic circumstances resulting from the use of weaponry upon innocent beings who, because of their misaligned stance, became caught in the cross fire, so to speak. It is tragic without a doubt that beautiful and innocent beings have suddenly and unexpectedly left the Earth Plane. I wish to assure you that they are always embraced in the healing love of the Creator through the assistance of Divine Beings within the inner planes. These Masters and Angelic Teams also are assisting those who grieve in shock upon the Earth as well. Know that healing is being enacted from the highest dimensions of Divine Presence.

Much fear fills the hearts of the masses every time a scenario of violent outbreak erupts, and it tarnishes the good work of those who promote peace and love in the world. Sorrow and grief spread vulnerability to those who do not foresee the turmoil through eyes of clarity, and so it saddens the hearts of us within the inner planes to know this violence occurs, as we all endeavor to uplift the hearts of all upon the Earth.

Never fail to send the families and friends of victims your healing love, for it is desperately needed in these circumstances. Also send love to the perpetrator of these crimes for they suffer greatly as well. Without judgment we seek to send love to all regardless of their stance in being.

Dear Ones, it is not for us to understand why these events unfold as they do, when the world is in dire need of healing aggression and violence. It is the breaking of hearts we see in these circumstances and I, Archangel Metatron, send legions of Angels to mend the spirits and souls of those devastated by the travesty of broken faith and trust. Do understand, we do all we may, and all that can be received by those who suffer continually in order to repair and heal the hearts, psyches, and minds of the many effected by this collective disruptive force weighing heavily upon the masses. All are affected when one is affected, as we exist within the Oneness of All That Is.

Dear Ones, please be assured you shall be safe in the world, and also throughout your journeys wherever your hearts lead you, so as to continue your great work and upliftment. Do not let discouragement stand in your way. Move onward in trust and in faith that All Is Well and So It Is.

22

Always By Your Side

THE MEASURE OF WHO YOU ARE and what you are is beyond your mind's ability to perceive through thought or imagination. Your presence here upon the Earth is immeasurable in that the flow of continual light and love are moving through you out into the world. Your love is infinite as well as immeasurable due to your being a constant and continual source of light to all. Please be assured that no amount of distraction or upset can hinder this flow, for it is who and what you are here in the world and within the inner planes.

Please be assured you are always in my protection, and never fear external circumstances that pervade your stance in being, for you are here as Messengers of Light to uplift the hearts and minds of many. And in this knowing I, Archangel Metatron, shall be by your side day and night to see you through any and all adverse experience, to carry you through without sorrow or discouragement so that you may continually manifest your gifts and love out into the world to fulfill your purpose in being.

Now is a time of great disruption and fear as the dark influences upon humanity pervade those of innocence and also those who are aware of this presence upon the Earth. Do not fear, as this only opens you to these energetic pathways of dark intent. Always remain in trust and love, for then no one nor no thing may harm you as you maintain alignment with the Truth of All That Is.

And what does this mean to be truly and completely aligned with Divine Presence? It means you exist in a state of total trust and confidence that all is unfolding so that everyone's experience in the world is perfect for their chosen pathway. Even though some have yet to come into alignment, they are still in their process of finding the truth within their own being, and this is not to be judged nor disputed, as each being has their own means to discover their internal stance of love within. Do not fear for others, nor fear among those of like mind, as all is within the loving embrace of Creator's Essence in Being.

Should you experience fear, or other energetic emotionality that disrupts your alignment, do not be concerned. Only breathe into the depth of your being and intend to realign with your inner knowing so that you regain your divine stance in being. There are no repercussions for this, only the need to once more move into alignment until this becomes your constant state in being. You will not become vulnerable to harm for momentary lapses due to distracting lower vibrational states. You simply return to the place within that exists in love and acceptance of All That Is.

Please be advised to receive my loving protection within your Being so that you can relax and enjoy your lives free of fear and doubt, for I, Archangel Metatron, will always be by your side and So It Is.

23

Peace Be With You

PEACE BE WITH YOU, Dear Ones, for all the world's turmoil and sorrow, there is always the Light of the Creator's Grace within you and everyone. And in time, as you experience it, this turmoil and sorrow shall come to pass. To experience peace amid the disruptive forces upon the Earth can be challenging when you see much pain and suffering around you and sometimes within your own lives. However, this is not to be of concern, for now I, Archangel Metatron, shall fortify and strengthen your resolve to exist within the chaos in a peaceful and knowing state of being.

Dear Ones, forever and ever there has been only the loving presence of the Creator, and now we see the results of free will choice from all manifest beings who are exploring different vantage points to view reality based upon their own truths formed from illusion, and lower emotional frequencies that pervade the collect mind. And so I say to you, do not despair in allowing the expression of various elemental forces that may manifest, so as to bring greater balance into the world and lives of its inhabitants.

Now we see there is much work to do in conscious thought intention to bring the inner peace into our external reality, so as to provide a basis for all to gravitate to in times of suffering and painful realization that the world is out of balance, and that Mother Earth shall manifest means to clear this critical mass field of negativity from her Being and Soul. She wishes only for those upon her to survive and ascend along with her. However, it is all right that some may become entangled in the downturn of events, as they shall be liberated through pathways chosen specifically of their own making. Do not grieve nor fear for others whose paths take a seemingly different direction, for they shall be free when they have completed their own process in their own time and So It Is.

Now is time to concentrate upon the avenues of light pouring forth into the world, to heal and transform those who open their hearts to their true nature, for they shall be redeemed through the goodness of their true expression in being. Fear not, for what comes to others, is not the same experience that the Lightworkers have chosen for themselves, as they are ambassadors of good will to this Earthly plane. Some have left this dimension to work within the inner planes to assist in Earth's Ascension, and some are within this dimensional plane to anchor the energetic transmissions from those within, who send their brilliance and soulful expression into this world because of their devotion to all upon the Earth and This Is So.

More of this love and more of this conscious ability to manifest Light and uplifting expressions of Grace penetrate the very consciousness of Mother Earth and all who reside upon and within her Being. Be it known that on this day, I, Archangel Metatron, Bless all Beings who receive my message through energetic connectivity by those of loving heart and So It Is.

24

Be Like The Sun

TODAY WE SEE many people in a state of confusion and anger, and so it is imperative that all Lightworkers focus upon their own ability to send light into the world without judgment of who and where it is to be received. For all beings are in need of loving light energetic transmissions of Grace.

When you encounter someone who is filled with angst and grief due to their entanglement with the world's chaos, then you have the opportunity to send them your love, which will unconsciously draw them into greater alignment with the Truth of their own Being. You see when someone is sent love, they know this on every level of their being, and this love permeates their cellular makeup physically and energetically, and they then feel enlivened and also feel simply loved. This simple act can move mountains, my friends, and can also redirect their focus into a more loving and understanding stance.

You see, Dear Ones, this love is healing and given freely in the knowing that All Is Well, and that they too may exist in love. Your love to them reminds them of their own inner love and helps to bring this out into their external existence. Everyday is an opportunity to send out love, for you see, life is an adventure and a challenge in that we have the choice to live our best lives, and in so doing we create a more loving world.

This simple act, that is almost indiscernible to those who receive it, is of immense importance, for there is nothing else in this world that is more powerful than love.

We need to understand this gift of giving love is also an opportunity for us to exist in love always, which is of course healing to our own selves and our own souls. Dear Ones, be like the sun. Be like the Sun. Be like the Sun giving freely loving light to all, so that all beings grow in this light to express their own inner light out into the world. Be like the Sun. And So It Is.

It is not for us to judge one another or anyone who may seem impossible to love. For love heals all without question, without doubt, and this love is the answer to all that ails the world and those who suffer within it. Love. Love. Love is the answer as you have heard numerous times, and yet do you really understand how this is true?

This truth prevails, as it is the only energetic transmission that can penetrate hate and sorrow and vengeance and greed. Love conquers all lower vibrational emotional states of being. Trust and It Is So. For this is a testament for All who reside upon the Earth, and the entire Universe and Beyond. And So It Is.

25

Need To Understand That All Is Well Within The Coming Changes On The Earth

SOON THERE IS TO BE A TIME of reckoning that shall define those who shall ascend, from those wishing to journey onward through the halls of dualistic behavior, and I, Archangel Metatron, shall assist All upon their chosen path. No One is abandoned, and so, Dear Ones, do not weep nor be concerned, for the well being of all is unfolding into the loving arms of God among the various multitudinous avenues that lead back into the conscious presence of Creator's Grace.

Be not afraid, I say once again, for the changes upon your horizon are many and shall appear as dark and foreboding, when in fact they are simply a form of transitional appearance to cleanse the darkness from the souls of those who wish to be free. The time of transition is tumultuous indeed upon the planet, and I wish for you to prepare for the coming turmoil through your knowing that All Is Well upon the Earth. She ascends into the higher dimensions of Being, so that all frequencies not resonate with the Earth changes, falls away to be redirected into other spheres of existence appropriate to their chosen path of experience.

Now, please be aware that the dramas unfolding in your external experience are only for the outplay of karmic episodes so as to elevate humanity as a whole, while also address the personal reflective experience of the individual, which is varied and unique. While humanity as a whole shall appear to suffer, individuals shall have their own unique expression of transformative experience that will move them forward into the knowing of their own expression of Truth.

Now, be aware that your personal expression of experience shall be one of ease, so long as you do not become entangled in the fear and trauma happening out in the world. This does not mean you shall not have a part to play in helping others who appear lost. It means you shall continue your Lightwork of compassion out into the external world to uplift those who suffer and are confused due to their lost stance.

It is only for those to know that All Is Well, who have grown into this awareness, for this state of consciousness is one that arrives when one is ready to receive their inner truth. Do not feel alarmed for those who appear lost, for they are in their own process and shall eventually become aligned with Divine Purpose once again, when it is the perfect time for them to attune and elevate their awareness of the Unity of All That Is.

Please let it be known that although you may see great upset and suffering, you shall be safe within the protection of your own knowing for All Is Well. Understand here what is said, so that you may accept the external circumstance, while maintaining your own space of peaceful, loving presence. Know that All Is Well. Please understand that there is no one and no thing that is separate from Creator's loving embrace. Now, understand that All Is Well, regardless of external appearances, for Peace and Love and Joy and Compassion reigns within the hearts of those who choose to open their Hearts to Christed Loving Light and So It Is.

26

Find A Way To Become
Your Own Best Friend

WHEN IN DOUBT, Dear Ones, of your stance in the world regarding how well you feel about who you are, you may come into question your own ability to ascend along with your earthly sphere. You may wish to pause and reflect upon your own state of being in that there are numerous ways to see yourself as a Being of Love and Light. Know you are deserving of all good fortune that comes your way, for you are the quintessential vibratory illustration of what it is to be in the physical, while also embodying your soulful expression of Divine Presence.

There are ways in which to solidify your self belief that you are indeed ascending, as there are no bells or whistles to alert you to the shifts and changes that are occurring within your being and soul. Trust that you are moving along at an accelerated pace and may experience only subtle changes, rather than profound and dramatic shifts of awareness so that you hardly notice the differences on a day to day basis as they feel like a natural and easy progression of growth.

Be that as it may, yes, there are moments when you have illumination or increased clarity around a particular event that opens you to greater perception. However, for the most part, the ascension process is gentle and easy to integrate into your daily existence so that you continue grounded within your physical reality. Know that I, Archangel Metatron, am with you every step of the way, and also know that all of Creator's loving guidance and support within the inner planes of higher dimensional expression, are also with you in assisting your upliftment and evolution into higher and higher states of awareness of Creator's Universe. For what exists within your Being is nothing less that the Oneness of All That Is and what exists outside yourselves is a perfect reflection of your inner state in Being.

Thus you may align more and more with the Divine Truth of your being through your external experience which avails to you a sense of flow and ease. If you experience discord or dissonance, then you may see what does not align in your experience, and consciously correct your stance to move into love, and out of judgment or fear or doubt. Always rectifying your stance into one of love does sound simple. However, to become aware of elements within your being that are not aligned is the challenge, for then you will become more conscious of what does not reflect your inner truth and love.

And so, Dear Ones, continue your journey in confidence that you will be assisted in this knowing by those who love you within the inner planes, as well as those who present the challenges in your external reality. For those who appear discordant are actually a blessing in disguise, for they illuminate what needs to shift and change within your own being. Do be aware that you may call upon me, Archangel Metatron, for help with any issues that arise within your external reality, so that I may guide you into a larger perspective of what is transpiring so as to illuminate what awareness is called for your conscious recognition allowing you the knowing to more greatly align with your Inner Truth and So It Is.

27

Everyone Has Need To Take A Breath

ALWAYS A NEED to cooperate with those around you so that you may find a harmonious stance in Being. To be harmonious, while at the same time present in your truth, is the key to expressing effectively your light and also your wisdom. You see, Dear Ones, there is never a circumstance where you need to be 'on guard' so to speak, for you exist in a state of loving presence and this alignment shall always guard you from harm.

For you to offer your light and love to any circumstance is a natural unfoldment of your day's routine. Do think of it in this way, for you are now embodying the truth you have sought for so long. It has always been there, and so now that you are open to it, it is no longer necessary to resist situations where you once felt uncomfortable or threatened due to beliefs that others are holding. For you are nonreactive to accusations, distrust, or any other adverse energetic projection from those who have yet to come into alignment with their own truth.

You see now that you have arrived at a stance in existing in a loving state, there is nothing and no thing that can harm you so as to alter your ability to respond in love to all manner of things unfolding throughout your daily existence. Always the look and presence of love shall neutralize any lower vibrational energetic exchange belonging to another, for you shall know within your heart that Love is always the answer.

So easy to say, yet not so easy to do when someone is projecting their own fear and insecurity upon your being. You feel within your own being the memory and remnants of past insecurities and fears of your own. Now I, Archangel Metatron, suggest you call upon me when you feel inadequate to meet the challenge of aligning in love, for I shall clear your angst and fear to bring you into perfect response for every challenging situation you may encounter as you move through your day and through your entire existence. For I, Archangel Metatron, see you as perfect, and when energetic confrontations cause you to be pulled out of loving presence, I shall gently move you back into this alignment if only you can remain mindful of this when a distressing event or situation occurs.

For you are Divine, Dears Ones. Of this there is no doubt. Do not fear if your reactive impulses arise, for this may happen from time to time when you are caught unawares, and then do call upon me to assist you, or you may simply take a breath and realign your heart and mind to regain your loving stance. You must remember you are human and have experienced the discord of much human experience within your psyche and soul, and so be patient with yourselves in resolving old reactive patterns of resistant defensive behaviors. In time this shall all fall away and So It Is.

28

Peace Becomes You

PEACE BECOMES YOU when you reside in the constant focus of conscious presence within the momentary movement along your timeline. When you exist within the perimeters of time and space then you receive the experience of becoming the presence of peace, for there is nothing else to perceive when the mind does not wonder into fantasy or worry or distraction from the moment of simply being.

You see, Dear Ones, peace is a state of being when there is nothing to concern your thoughts, your mind, with what is not present in your experience. It is the distractions of the mind which create suffering, for you see the mind wishes to control your fate through its creative process, regardless of whether you are conscious of your thoughts or not. For the creation of thoughts stemming from fear or worry or doubt or any other form of distressing source, can not only create the manifestation of these concerns into your reality, they also can create your behavioral response to them, and this is illusive. For you see there is only in reality the present moment to experience, and everything else is of the mind's creation.

It is not wrong to think creatively when your thoughts are aligned with divine purpose in becoming more attuned, or more productive, or more present in your life. However, to think from a place of lower vibrational emotional discord is not of benefit in any way because you may feel that there are forces outside of your control which gives rise to fearful projections that create within your being much trepidation, and thus your thoughts move into beliefs that this is real and outside of your circumstance of control. You see this is the creation of illusion, and you may experience illusive events that are not real in any sense outside of your own volition.

And so, Dear Ones, do be aware that this form of identification with your beliefs and your thoughts are not for your highest good when they do not reflect your true divinity. For now, you being of higher vibrational stance do not have the luxury to indulge in frivolous thoughts and fantasies, because your power to manifest more rapidly within your conscious thought intention is a responsibility to acknowledge at this time in your development.

Contrary to popular belief, lower vibrational thought forms, derived from fear or fantasy to amuse, can cause you grief in that they are created from a sense of lack in Being. Without fully devoting yourself to the expression of truth and trustful knowing that all is well, will only deter or even derail your divine flow and direction in life. Never indulge in thoughtless self recriminations or harsh judgments upon others, for this creates more illusive reactivity to external circumstance, which will eventually manifest as an obstruction in your development.

Do not fear when unconscious thoughts creep into your mind, for they often are not of your making, but only information existing within the collective of the earthly plane. Such thoughts that do not originate within your own mind can be a distraction as well, for some part of your being is attuning to these vibrational thought forms. It is easy to allow these to penetrate your consciousness, and so I, Archangel Metatron, shall assist you in uplifting your frequency so as to elevate the level of perceived information.

For it is true that throughout Creator's Universe you may connect into higher knowing, clarity, and perception of the truth of your reality upon the Earth and the experience there, without the clutter of lower vibrational thoughts intruding upon your mind and soul. Know that this is so when you simply ask me for help in this matter, and become a constant source of Light upon the Earth so that you shine throughout your Dimensional Presence.

29

We Are One And One Is All

NOW DEAR ONES, for most of you present within this discourse, you will find that you are evolving and growing in new ways. Your perception of life in general is richer and deeper, and so you may always feel that you are in the flow of divine presence upon this earthly plane. Be advised that there are numerous means of expression that are specific to your own qualities and interests that emanate through your conscious choices. Everyone here who integrates this discourse should know that they are well on their way within their own ascension process that coincides with the ascension process of the Earth.

This is a beautiful thing to behold, for you may conceive inspiration in new ways daily due to the intake of various higher dimensional thought patterns that exist in the higher dimensional realms of existence, for you are of a growing frequency of continual expansion. These patterns shall realign your lower thought patterns with higher vibratory expressions, so that your old, habitual patterns generated from fear and other forms of fear and lack, are extinguished from your heart and mind. And so know that you are receiving the Grace from the Creator that will move you forward requiring only your intent to let go and move forward in Truth and absolute Trust.

Dear Ones, there is no reason to doubt this process or to doubt your journey of Ascension. Simply be present and breath fully and relax into the divine flow of your daily life trusting All Is Well. And I say this once more, as you need to be assured often, that despite all the world's confusion and turmoil, Divine Grace is present manifesting in multitudinous ways throughout everyone and everything. For those who suffer still, for they have not awakened to the creation of their own thought projections, are still in the process of growth, for eventually they will awaken in their own time and the experience of their suffering will guide them into divine alignment.

As we have discussed this phenomenon before, you see this is so, within and without the third dimensional existence. And yet there is more you may understand in time that will allow you to take solace in the knowing that All Is Well. This understanding will occur eventually when you are capable to perceive your current experience of the world through higher dimensional thought patterns, for they will create a sense of Unity of All Things upon and within the earthly realm. Without this understanding, the world appears as a sorrowful and sad state of being, when it actually is a playground for earthly drama allowing everyone their free will choice to experience what they require to evolve and grow within, so that they eventually become aligned once more with their Creator source in Being.

Do know that in time, as you perceive it, there are numerous ways to alleviate concern and acquired suffering from the global manifestation of pain and suffering. One way is to simply trust that All Is Well. Another way is to become a source of continual love and compassion for the entire world and all the individual components within it. There is only One in Truth, and there is only One in existence. The components that are suffering still are simply exercising their free will choice so as to experience what they require in order to learn more about who they truly are, and this is allowed here and actually everywhere throughout the Universe.

Even though some may wish to define the natural order of the Universe as one of chaos and random acts based on happenstance in nature, this is not so. The Universe is highly organized through the conscious intention of all Beings within it, and the divine essence of the Creator oversees all experience, for it is the One Creator of All that is the One experiencing All, through all manifest beings throughout the Universe and beyond. So you see Dear Ones there is no separation in reality, only millions upon billions of soul expressions of the Divine Presence of the One. Know this Truth within your Heart and Soul and So It Is.

30

Letting Go Of The Past

SEQUENCES OF VIBRATORY PATTERNS within the Heart and Mind and Soul determine one's perception of reality, and so it is known among Lightworkers that they may rely upon this mode of perception as one of true clarity in Being. For you see, Dear Ones, there is only this moment within this field of luminosity and presence, so that you perceive your own truth in being.

So be it to say, that when you are in dire financial stress, or the emotional stress of lower vibrational expression, you are indeed in dire entanglement of fear and doubt. Do not hesitate to call upon me, Archangel Metatron, for I shall know how to assist you in your time of confusion, for you are residing within your past perception of reality, and so you do hold onto the fears present in the past. Reckless abandonment of prior lifetime karmic repercussions of neglected responsibility to yourself and others return for just compensation, and so I, Archangel Metatron, can not only assist you in moving beyond these karmic blocks, but also cleanse your energetic records of these past grievances, and So It Is.

Fearful stance of surviving financially and or physically, is not one belonging to those who reside in the truth of their own being, for they know that all is well, and that they are supported and protected in all ways required to meet their needs upon this earthly plane of existence. Also, those residing in truth shall enjoy the abundance and ease of existing in this beautiful sphere of reality. Trust and it is so, Dear Ones, for the beliefs and anxiety around issues of lack and insecurity are resulting manifestations due to past experience of dualistic entanglement, and also from traumatized perception that has yet to be recognized and cleared from your being.

And so I, Archangel Metatron, shall not only assist you in clearing the past traumatized experience, I also shall assist those who ask of me, to heal all aspects of their prior lifetime traumatized perception due to culturally indoctrinated experience. Be it known to those who read here, that all past grievances may be healed within their Hearts and Souls, for through their openness to receive Creator's Loving Grace, they are Blessed and also cherished by the Beings of Divine Light and So It Is.

Never delay to release and let go of all past angst and sorrow for this is illusive, resulting from old paradigm systematic belief structures and dualistic suffering. Dear Ones, now is not the time to wallow in past grievances. Now is the time to Trust and hold sacred the Truths given here. For Thine is the Kingdom of Heaven upon the Earth and So It Is. Peace be with you in the knowing that All Is Well.

31

Seeing The Beauty In All Things

FOR ALL WHO EXIST upon and within the Earth, life shall continue to evolve despite the horrific news coming through the media, and although much fear and terror is daily reported, there is much to celebrate in the ever increasing Light and Love flowing into the spherical environment of Earth. Dear Ones, find in your daily lives beauty in the smallest acts of kindness so your focus remains upon that which is positive and loving. When amid the global sorrow and chaos, it is important to remember to trust All Is Well and focus upon what beauty surrounds you in your lives, be it a plant or a rainbow or the pristine quality of water.

By keeping your focus upon that which is beautiful and true, your heart and mind remain in Divine Flow. Nothing is benefited through attuning to the grief and suffering of the world. So be it to say that when sending love out into the world, you may find that focusing upon what is positive shall assist you in keeping your vibratory stance of Christed Loving Light. And this will prevail and emanate out into the world without need of suffering the collapse of old paradigm systems.

By attuning to the beauty and grace you see in the world, your energetic fields are invulnerable to being lowered into the third dimensional collective field of suffering. It is correct to maintain a high vibrational stance when anchoring great light and healing love into the world. Feeling sorrow does not contribute one iota of help to the collective third dimensional state of being. It not only does not feel good, it also allows great sorrow to enter your field of being due to your attunement to it. From a lowered emotional stance, your love is not as effective in healing yourself or others, and so do intend to attune to the beauty in life so that undue suffering is not yours to experience.

You have already ascended into higher dimensions in Being and so you need not suffer anymore due to the conditional stance of those entangled in dualistic behaviors. You see, Dear Ones, you may experience joy and beauty and truth amid the third dimensional confusion, as you are no longer residing within those frequencies. All you need focus upon is the love within your Being and thus unconditionally express this love out into the world fearlessly to All in existence. This is a great act of compassion and a great act of presence so as to uplift the collective through your heartfelt intent to heal the planet and all upon her.

Envision your world as one of peace and one of plenty and one of harmony and exist as though It Is So Now. This projection does much to uplift the planet's vibratory flow and so do not become entangled in the sorrow of the world. Accept that all is well and that your vision of World Peace is manifest so as to live from this place now. You may feel this is impossible; however, it is important for Lightworkers to realize the immense power of your thoughts as they are the source of origin of all manifestation in the world. So do not despair for those who suffer as I, Archangel Metatron, again tell you All Is Well. You may wish to call upon me for support to align to Creator's loving presence and So It Is.

32

Listening and Acting From The Heart

NOW DEAR ONES, it is a time of great knowing that through recognition and rectification, you become more attuned to the Divine Alignment of Creator's Ascension Path. There is no need to chastise one's self due to minor mistakes and temporary confusion. There is only your expanding awareness of following your heart's knowing in every moment, without becoming distracted by those who do not resonate with your divine purpose. For your purpose is to fulfill your own healing, and then extend your abilities to others who are open to receive.

How do you know who is ready to receive when approached by someone, you may ask? You will know through your heart's recognition of another open heart, not so much by what is said, as by the intent of the person you reside with to truly communicate through loving intent. There is the innocent response to assist everyone you encounter and this is admirable; however, it is also a detriment to you and this person, when they are not ready to receive in that it creates confusion for you both.

When someone is not open to healing and guidance, they resist and reject your intent to be helpful, and are incapable of hearing your truth as you speak and act. And so do discern who is residing within their heart space and who is not before you interact with them, as they will not display interest in your spiritual pursuits. Suffice it to say, being in a state of open heart does not mean to always give of yourselves when you encounter someone else who does not share this stance. To be on guard or judgmental of another is not what I intend for you to experience, however, being attuned to your Divine Flow is. And when in divine flow, you will naturally sense the sincerity of those around you, and will only interact when you feel moved through your heart space.

Being in a state of readiness to always assist another, is not necessarily the same as being in a state of listening to your heart. For when you feel moved to speak, it is because your soul and heart and mind is knowing that the energetic transmission of love may flow unimpeded to another due to their openness. When you sense someone is not open, then you will not feel the impulse to help them or offer guidance, or even speak of your ability to heal. This discourse is only for those who are ready, and only your heart can know for certain that someone is. And so wait, Dear Ones, until you are asked to expound upon spiritual matters of the heart. Wait until you feel someone is sincere and genuine in wishing to enquire of your gifts and love so that you remain in divine flow at all times.

It is simply time to fine tune your senses and abilities, to navigate the world without entangling yourselves in the dark influences moving through those who remain in the dark, so to speak. Please be advised to always wait and feel into your heart space before lending your helping hands Dear Ones. Thus, you will not expend unnecessary energy to those who cannot appreciate your gifts. Be advised to always listen to your heart impulse in giving your Truth before acting, so that no harm is done to yourselves in becoming an object of ridicule or rejection. Thus, only those who are seeking Truth receive your assistance and So It Is.

33

Arrival Of A Peaceful Planet

TODAY OF ALL DAYS, we seek to enliven our quest to heal the Earth and one another so that we may exist in a state of well-being and peace now and into the future. For it is known to all Lightworkers that there is a plague upon this planet that is doing great harm to the environment and to the beings who exist here. Within the hearts and minds of those who perpetrate these misdeeds, we find they have disconnected from their true knowing of their loving presence within, and so I, Archangel Metatron, shall release All Innocent Beings who suffer from the wrong doing of criminal acts all terror and fear and pain and suffering and also death, so that they may rise unencumbered, by the horrific injustice and slaughter of lives upon the continental plates, and also in the oceans where aquatic life is suffering and dying due to serious imbalances generated by the hands of humanity.

I, Archangel Metatron, ask all Lightworkers today to send their love out into the world, to release all grief and pain and suffering from those who suffer in innocence, due to the vile acts of the few who control the wealth of the world, and also for those who grieve this travesty of incomparable hideous attacks upon mankind, and also upon animal and plant Beings who are destroyed in these destructive efforts by those who will not ascend, as they are not aligned with Divine Purpose.

Although not everyone is aligned for Ascension at this juncture, everyone will eventually ascend when they have completed their experience of living in dualistic vibratory manifestation.

Envisioning a world where all Beings are Free, and all creatures and manifest forms of Being, whether aquatic or of plant nature, may reside in harmonious, peaceful coexistence as One in the awareness of being expressive of their own Truth. You see, Dear Ones, without the intent to do harm, everything changes in the third-dimensional plane, so as to create a world of high vibrational existence where only loving intent exists. Without ill will, the entire planet would evolve and ascend, and so it is necessary for those who cannot resonate with the higher frequencies penetrating the magnetic sphere of your planet, to be lovingly escorted to other planets resonate with the lessons they seek to learn, which will eventually allow them to ascend as well.

There are reasons why this planetary shift is happening at this time and so do not feel alarmed as though the world is at an End. It is in fact embarking on a new beginning that will elevate the hearts and minds of those who seek a peaceful existence living in accord and generosity, among all who remain in residence upon the ascending Earth. This is cause for celebration, for after many eons of your time the outcome of continuous conflict and suffering is now reaching resolution, and there is to be no more pain and suffering in your lives, and there will be great love and beauty in your experience in living in this world of wonder and magnificence.

Do not be alarmed when outward appearances overwhelm your media outlets, as this imagery depicts the resulting effects of dire destruction and horrifying death of innocent lives due to the betrayal of those who have lost their way. The innocent shall be redeemed and uplifted and healed within the inner and outer planes and so take heart in this knowing that all will be rectified eventually, although it does not appear so to those simply looking at the outside world. Fear not, for All Is Well Dear Ones, and I, Archangel Metatron, embrace all who wish for Peace in the World and So It Is.

34

Today Is Always An Extraordinary Day

FOR MOST TODAY is just another day. However, for those who send light from their hearts into the world for healing all that creates discord upon the planet, today, is an opportunity to dissolve darkness and fear in the hearts of humanity, and to also shed light upon all who are in discord with their inner truth. Recent events have seemingly curtailed progress of a spiritual nature; however, this is not entirely so, as much karma has played out to clear past grievances, and open new pathways into a deeper and truer understanding of the ascension process.

For those who do not shrink from their responsibility to assist humanity and all life forms in thriving and evolving is the promise of recompense in the course that lies ahead. For they shall lead others through their exemplary behavior and through their stance of embodying Christed Presence emanating into the hearts of the many they encounter by merely being in their countenance.

Do not be disturbed by those who would scorn your truthful expression, for they are in fear of losing their own sense of stability and security built from culturally indoctrinated beliefs that do not embrace the spiritual process of growth and illumination. It is all right that they do not, for in time they shall experience growth through their own perspective when they are ready. So as not to confuse you Dear Ones, the light you emanate out to others does have an effect regardless of the receptivity of an individual, for Light penetrates all things without discrimination.

You see there are numerous ways in which you may direct your healing light into the environment in which you live, and into the world in areas of focus that are in need of healing. And so I, Archangel Metatron, shall assist your heartfelt intentions wherever they may be directed, so as to empower your ability to send out greater and greater amounts of Light into the lives of All. Thus, there is greater impact for those who you wish to help through your compassionate stance and So It Is. Always be aware that you have great power and capacity of infinite nature to give of your own heart, for there is no end to the amount you may give. Just as the nature of the Universe is infinite, so is the Love within your own Heart. Trust and It is So.

35

Whether Near Or Far All Is One

TODAY IS ANOTHER OPPORTUNITY to serve the highest good of All, and so, Dear Lightworkers, do realize that not a day passes that does not benefit from your loving presence through your divine thought intentions directed at those who require assistance and healing. You see there are many avenues to experience that are of eloquent expressions of Grace. And so do know that any and all wishes for divine assistance is responded to through your intent to heal and repair the planet, as well as those in need of loving support, in order to recover and heal from traumatized perceptions in being.

Be it far from your heart's embrace, no distance is too great to send your healing love, and so do not feel incapable of affecting the outcomes of dire stress and sorrow happening near and far. For there are no divisions throughout time and space, only the expressions of multitudinous life forms existing upon the planet united through the Oneness of All that Is.

Dear Ones, be assured your loving intent is received through your heart's connectivity to Divine Grace, and the appropriate response is given through dimensional means of energetic effects upon your area of focus by the Beings of Light delegated to oversee your cause. 'Effect' is meant to mean, that the energetic formation of healing love is dispersed to the areas you ask to be healed, and so there is no need to doubt that this is so each and every time you ask for healing assistance. The 'effect' created is bound by the parameters of the openness one is capable of receiving, and so no amount of healing energy can completely heal one when they do not receive with open heart the dispersement of energetic energies 'showered' upon them, so to speak. And so it is not always evident that healing has transpired, however, always healing has been enacted to some degree, and so even a small amount received is really quite significant in view of transformative energetic transmissions of Light, which is powerful beyond all imaginings.

This is not to say that one does not have control over whether or not they receive Divine Grace. It is to say that although one's heart may not be completely open to loving light, the amount of openness they do have is determined through their own volition, and so it is karmically appropriate to offer this healing regardless of their conscious permission to do so. For to receive any amount of Grace, is determined not only on the level of physical existence, but also on Soul level. Many who may not consciously determine the choice to benefit from this energetic healing may unconsciously allow it, due to their Soul predilection for growth and So It Is.

Permission to heal another being is Supreme and to acknowledge one's conscious choice is necessary in most cases, however, when dealing with the healing intent for many Beings who are in a form of jeopardy, it is permitted to shower them with healing Grace if they give permission on their Soul level. And yes, there are Souls who occasionally who do not allow this, however, for the most part, Soul Beings do wish to receive healing when offered.

It is advised to preference your loving intent always with the phase that you already may utilize, which is, "...that it should be for the highest and best good of All." Thus, permission is granted to the Light Beings of Benevolent Intent to make the wisest appropriate karmic choice in assisting your prayers, for when you intend to call upon us for assistance in healing various situations and beings, we do respond immediately and know this is so. Know This Is So, for we are the Legions of Light Beings who reside within your Hearts and Minds in the Oneness of All That Is. Blessed Be those who seek the Kingdom of Heaven for it is within Your very Heart and Soul.

36

Finding Peace In Loving Acceptance

PEACE IS MORE than a word, an idea, a concept. It is the presence of heartfelt knowing of one's own Soul Presence. To be in a state of Peace is to be in a state of Grace, so that any and all things manifesting into your existence is accepted with the knowing that All Is Well. There is no known ability that creates peace within your being other than to exist with an open loving heart and always reside in that space. This is peace, Dear Ones. This is Peace. For peace is the state achieved when you do not entangle yourself in outcomes and fear of what comes next. It is a state of Trust and a state of allowing your soul to manifest in all its knowing, and so do not try to achieve peace, for it cannot be achieved through any means other than existing in a state of loving acceptance of all things as they are.

You see, Dear Ones, much is spoken about in terms of achieving peace in the world and within ourselves, and actually, because it is a state of being, it cannot be achieved through external means. It is a condition one experiences when feeling true compassion and love for All. How does this come about you ask when there is so much strife in the world that we witness everyday? It comes about through your unconditional acceptance of all things as they are, without resistance to anyone or anything, be it an idea, belief, or concept.

You see peace comes to those who unconditionally accept the stance and free will expressions of all Beings as they so choose to experience in the world. And yes, it is difficult to see the wrongful choices of those who harm others in some way, be it slight or of immense proportions. However, when you understand that loving acceptance is a stance of being in a state of unconditional love for all, you understand you are feeling love for the Oneness integral within every being, regardless of what choice they make. For we are One Dear Ones, and loving everything and everyone as they are is actually a gesture of loving oneself unconditionally.

You see through this perspective there is no separation in being, and although we may be in distress due to the horrific outcome created through wrongful misaligned actions, it is still an expression of free will choice, and this is the key to existing in love here in this dimensional plane of dualistic existence. You see now, that all who suffer the consequences of the wrongful actions are not to be judged, for karmic choices manifest in multitudinous ways of expression. It is not for us to judge when we cannot know the reasons why someone could harm another. It is for Us to send out love to All without separation, so as to heal the entirety of the planetary consciousness, as the light dissolves the darkness everywhere, and in your time you shall experience the difference you make in residing in a stance of peaceful loving acceptance of All That Is.

Know this, Dear Ones, your hearts and minds focused upon peaceful and loving acceptance is the key to create the changes needed within the hearts and minds of the collective consciousness of humanity. Working from the inside out is the process in which this can occur. It is said, that many understand that change happens from within our own Beings and this is so. Dear Ones, This Is So. Peace Be within you and may every moment of your existence be filled with the unconditional Love of All. And So It Is.

37

Only The Loving Heart Heals Conflict

TO EVERYONE upon your planet, be it known that Love is the key to eternal salvation, so as to be free of all entangled existence of earthly dire reactive behaviors. For all should be aware that Love is not only the key, love is the only answer to all problems and wounding within the hearts of All Beings and So It is. Love heals All. Love frees All. Love is the energetic presence of the Truth of the Creator within all who allow this Grace to manifest fully within their being.

Sovereign rights are violated when one accuses another of wrong doing without emanating the truth of love. So when a situation occurs where there is conflictual reactive energies in play, know that the way clear of this, is to move into the heart center and emanate the Love from within your Being. From this stance one may understand the cause of the conflict, as they are able to disentangle their emotional response, and see the situation in clarity without personally identifying with the conflict.

Listen to your hearts, Dear Ones. Know that this is the only avenue that will bring resolution to any conflictual matter or concern, for only from this place may one create a better stance as to what is called for in order to resolve the situation. Striving to heal a situation of conflict through reason and understanding is not enough. Only when united with a loving stance will dire opposition come to conclusion without hurt feelings and misinterpretations. You see, there is not any other avenue of expression that can penetrate the psyche without the means to communicate free of accusation and blame.

Only love can alleviate the need to be right simply due to egoic identification. When one emanates love, all personal afflictions dissolve and unity is achieved. This is the way to total understanding and genuine gestures of loving intent to 'clear the air' so to speak, without residual feelings of harm to one another. So you see, Dear Ones, I, Archangel Metatron, shall assist you when you are unable to move into your heart center through simply calling upon me to assist in the resolution of conflicts that you may encounter. I, Archangel Metatron, am at your beck and call, as I wish for you All to rise above egoic reactive behaviors, and emanate the Love you Truly Are and So It Is.

When one is able to maintain a loving stance in all situations that challenge one's egoic reactivity, then one may rise beyond the control of dualistic reactive behavior which shall free you from personally identifying with energies that create discord and disharmony in your lives. To remain steadfast within your loving heart is the key to liberation from all dualistic behaviors, which in turn gives way to the manifestation of your Soul Divine Presence, as the Heart may express its True Self and So It Is.

38

Truth Within Shall Guide You Always

EVERYWHERE YOU LOOK, everywhere you are, there is the essence of Truth. Truth is the expression of All existing within Creator's Universe and Beyond. Truth is your Divine Essence within your very Being. And so, Dear Ones, feel the truth within you whenever you find yourself to be in a state of confusion or conflict, as to what choice to make in responding to someone or some situation. Connecting into your own truth is achieved through the ability to disconnect from perceived expectations from without, and to instead listen to your heart from the stance of caring for all concerned.

To intuit within, the right choice to make in determining your direction in life; the right choice to make when others would misjudge or misunderstand you; the right choice to make in using your time so as to uplift yourself and others in activities that promote spiritual growth; the right choice to make when life is challenging in any way, so that you may always act from within the Truth in your Heart, and in this way express upliftment to all concerned.

It is not recommended that you belittle others for choosing activities or responses that you would not choose, for it is their free will to experience what choices they require in order to find their inner truth, even though it may appear to be taking them in the wrong direction. It is not for us to judge. It is not for us to determine what is right for another, for we all are in the process of finding the inner balance to experience our inner truth within. So, as we experience Inner Truth within ourselves, we then experience resolution to all difficult challenges outside of us.

Dear Ones, prepare to encounter much confusion in the world through this practice so that you always automatically respond to all situations and individuals through your loving heart. Navigating life's turmoil in this way is the answer to dissolve any suffering you might have incurred due to the dualistic expression of conflictual energies that abound upon the Earth. In this way of being you may discern when action is necessary, in order to express your truth without judging others, and thus your truth shall be received through the open receptivity of their own beings, without defensive behaviors being exchanged due to patterned response mechanisms.

Tumultuous times are ahead, Dear Ones, and I, Archangel Metatron, shall guide you through them so that you may understand how to navigate in the clear of all that may manifest in the world. Do not feel fear or repulsion, for this is a response due to not realizing the truth of what is being enacted upon the earthly plane of existence. Always remember to call on me when you experience anything indifferent to a loving stance, and I shall clear your hearts and minds of all illusion and fear so that you may continue to act from your heart space in every moment.

For to say there will be ease in all you experience from this heart space would be misleading, as it is natural for you to feel remorse and grief from past expressions of conflict in your lives. Now, it is time to allow these energetic grievances to be released from your entire Being and Soul, so that you may always respond without activating past pain and suffering in your life. To move forward without hesitation in the knowing that All Is Well, is to understand that you are not one to become entangled in the strife and karmic expression of dualism upon your planet.

I, Archangel Metatron, am at your side always to assist you in living your lives in joy and peace and love, regardless of external events happening around you, near or far. For you are Divine Beings, and it is known in the Heavens that you shall Ascend through your heartfelt desire to heal yourselves, and others who also wish for this magnificent transformation of your earthly presence and So It Is.

39

Be The Awareness Of Oneness
This Day And Always

TODAY OF ALL DAYS is not a day in particular, however, it is a day of reckoning all that transpires upon the Earth with all that transpires within the Inner Planes. As you see, Dear Ones, it is neither inner nor outer that defines your reality. There is, in fact, no separation between the two for what is within is reflected without. There is a need to understand this, for all separation is illusion.

And what does this mean in actuality? It means that energetic manifestations from within the divine flow of the Creator is brought into the physical environment of the your dimensional reality through benevolent action of loving thought intention in geometric design, so as to configure and construct biologic formation of all beings in existence here on Earth, and throughout the entire Universe and Beyond. It is so, that biologic manifestation is present everywhere you can possibly imagine, and then more so. For the infinite Universe is ever increasing and expanding in volume through manifest experience of multitudinous expressions of Creator's presence.

Now you see, without prior knowledge of this illusive imagery of separation, others around you may still be lost in this illusive circumstance. Beings are manifest in individualized expressions of unique qualities and gifts spread throughout all living beings, so as to experience unique expressions of Creator's abilities, talents, and perspectives. The uniqueness of each individualized being is due to genetic and also soul intent to experience one's karmic experience, and also one's ability to always grow and evolve within the framework of the individual's manifest reality.

This is not to be misunderstood here, for what I am saying is that an individual expression, although unique and of specific purpose, is still, all in all, one with all manifest reality in that the divine flow of the Creator is within and without all expression in Being. And, yes, there is only One Being here being expressed upon the Earth and throughout all eternal existence.

To exist is to Be, and to Be is to recognize your co-creative stance in being of this One Essence that allows Creator to experience continual growth and expansion through various means of individualized experience from a unique and solitary perspective. So that this unique expression is allowed individualized freedom of choice, thus the creative principle is enacted, and also may invent new and specialized vantage points existing within the Mind and Heart and Soul of the One Divine Essence and So It Is.

You see, Dear Ones, there is in reality no separation, only the illusion of separation due to the expansion of conscious learning and evolutionary development through the various aspects manifest of Creator's Being and Soul Essence. We each hold precious knowing within our hearts of this unity in divinity and we may at any point in time connect into this actualized stance in Being of One Heart and One Mind.

Without this awareness, the illusion of separation creates unnatural perception of the truth of our existence.

Thus, confusion and separation continue to create dual behavioral systems, and conflictual existence begins and ends there. So do not become entangled in this illusive perception in Being, as awareness of the Truth of our manifest reality unites us in Love and generous intent for All to live in harmonious co-existence and So It Is.

40

Know The Earth Receives Your Love

IT IS A BLESSED DAY TODAY, Dear Ones, in that today is another opportunity to assist your beautiful planet in its ascension process. For today is filled with the Earth's beauty and grace in Being, and you may consult her as to what she may need assistance with. Perhaps it is simply your gratitude in residing upon such a magnificent planet, or it could be she wishes for you to send her love and hold space for a peaceful existence. It may be one of many contributions she desires in order to evolve and ascend into the highest dimensions of Grace and Truth.

Be as it may, the Earth is also sending you and everyone love and peaceful emanations of joy and truth as she is Divine within her own presence, and may uplift your spirits through her beautiful expressions of natural manifestation, for this is who she is. And I say 'she' because the Earth is expressive of the feminine aspect first and foremost in her continual rebirth through cyclic repetitions of seasonal display.

You must realize that to be in service to Mother Earth is to be in service to your own self as well, as all who reside within and upon the Earth throughout all dimensions in being. For you see the inseparable nature of your planetary manifestation as One and One is All.

Do not despair the sorrow and darkness upon your planet, for its presence is fleeting like the leaves being blown from the trees in autumn time, a wistful phase of time passing so that new rebirth and new growth follows. Allow yourself to let go of all angst and sorrow due to the events upon your planet that appear to be of tragic proportions, as they are also fleeting. And hold to the vision of planetary peace and joy so that your Earth may ascend in this vision of Truth and Love.

Ours is to hold space for this beautiful planet so she may transition into the higher dimensions with ease. A letting go, so to speak, so that she no longer exists in the lower dimensional state of suffering and pain. The time is upon us now to rise in our vibrational expressions of love so to anchor and emanate the Truth within our Hearts and Souls. Thus the Earth is free to dissolve her entangled stance with polarized dimensionality, and ascend into the freedom and bliss of being within the Pure Light of the Creator, unencumbered by darkness.

Know this is so, and on this day do ask Mother Earth how to assist her, and ask this everyday. For simply a moment of your time spent on her behalf makes a wonderful difference, and So It Is.

41

To Be Free Is To Do No Harm

NOW WE SEE upon our earthly plane of existence that all Beings, great and small, are numerous expressions of Creator, and that all beings have the God Given Right to exist in peace and abundance so that they may experience the fullest expression of their manifest form as they have chosen, so as to gain greater wisdom and knowing of the Creator through that expression.

It is not for us to ever decide the fate of another being in this world, for each individual is Sovereign, and has the ability to choose their own fate in being upon the Earth. And so I address the belief that it is all right to kill animals for food consumption or amusement. How can this be right when all beings are manifest to express their freewill choice upon the Earth and everywhere throughout the Universe? It is not for one being to impose their intent of harm to another for self-serving purposes.

It is for all to coexist in harmonious unity and then all beings become an unfoldment of the divine flow in living and interacting together without even a hint of discord. Thus, All exist in Peace. You may feel this is high-minded thinking and not relevant to your current existence, and so I say to you, Dear Ones, high-minded thinking and high-minded coexistence is indeed the direction we shall embark upon. For it is only right to do so to remain in harmony with Mother Earth as she ascends into the higher dimensions of her Being, so as to exist in a state of Sovereign Expression within and without all manifestations of her being and So It Is.

Be it known that in order to ascend in harmonious evolutionary growth in a unified state of being, it is definitely important to not violate the freewill choice of another being, regardless of what and who they are. For to utilize another's sacred Being for the purpose of serving one's self, without regard for their wellbeing, is a violation of living freely upon the Earth and everywhere in Creator's Universe. Suffice it to say, it is recommended that all who wish to ascend with the Earth in her evolutionary journey must respect the knowing that the harming of any living being is not resonate with the energetic field of the ascension process.

Do not confuse Earth's Ascension with the individual paths an individual may take. It is possible to eat meat and to ascend at some transitory point in time; however, in order to ascend with the vibrational upliftment of the Earth's own ascension path, it is essential that you 'do no harm' to anyone, in any form. It is, of course, excused if any harm comes to a being when one is reacting in self-defense. Although, any being living in harmonious flow, will not experience this need to react, as nothing will harm them, for they harm no one themselves. When one consciously does no harm to any other being, there are no karmic repercussions of harm to one's self to experience.

You see, Dear Ones, it is advised to live your life free of ever creating misfortune or grief or pain for anyone, as the refinement of our existence depends upon the commitment and devotion to 'do no harm.' Thus, you are aligned with Creator's Divine Purpose in Being and So It Is.

42

Take Care To Heal Your Own Self

SPIRITUAL DEVELOPMENT comes from the belief that everyone is on a journey of individualized experience, whence come the realizations necessary to grow into higher dimensional awareness and presence of Loving Light. It is said that all who embark upon a pathway of light are to eventually arrive at an enlightened state. This much is true; however, it is also true that along the way soul travelers encounter obstacles and obstructions that hinder their development. For those who feel they are not progressing please call upon me, Archangel Metatron, for I shall assist you in clearing these blocks, and also healing the wounds that have created them and So It Is.

Do know that you are also capable of clearing your own maladies when you feel less than energetic and healthy, for you also have the ability to intend to release and heal all forms of detrimental experience and residual effects stemming from them. It is not difficult to do, Dear Ones. Simply invoke the intention to release all obstructing energetic blocks that hinder your ascension growth and then intend that this take place throughout your entire Being and Soul. If there is something that requires your conscious awareness of what is needed to clear, then you may spontaneously experience an image or memory of this affect. Thus, you are able to let it go through your cognizant recognition of that experience, allowing the release of what needs to be acknowledged consciously.

Do become aware that there may be obstructions at times that require the assistance of another healer who has an area of expertise, such as an acupuncturist or a nutritionist or a physician of traditional means. For there are numerous resources to draw from in your healing journey, so it is important to discern what is called for in order for you to heal a particular malady or hindrance to your well being. So know the importance of discernment in choosing what means best suits your needs in order to heal and let go.

It is advised to incorporate energetic conscious intention when involved in healing through external resources, so that the internal stance is open to releasing the core energetic obstruction generated from experience that has manifested emotionally, mentally, or physically.

Sometimes it is not enough to simple intend to release what is creating blocks in your development and sometimes it may be. This is for you to determine through attuning yourself to the issue at hand bringing greater awareness as to what you need to heal for a particular concern, or a particular obstructing energetic traumatized experience.

You see, Dear Ones, it is not enough to simply ask for healing sometimes, when more action is required to relieve oneself of problematic standstill. Suffice it to say, that in actuality there is never standstill, so to speak, as your health throughout all your energetic and physical bodies is either in a state of blossoming, increasing in vitality and spiritual growth, or it is in a state of stagnant decay. While you may be practicing good eating habits and exercise, there can sometimes be extenuating circumstance that interferes in your overall health, and this is due to past grievances that are contained within your being that have not been released, and so they can be a source of energetic imprinting upon your bodily tissues that have yet to physically manifest.

So it is good to enquire what past traumatized experiences you still contain within your field of Being so it may be released and healed prior to manifesting as a physical imbalance. Do not be frightened of your present condition, for if you are addressing current health issues then you are aware of what needs are essential for your healing. And if you feel completely healthy you may also wish to explore past traumatic energetic obstructions that need to be cleared so as to bring balance to your entire being.

Whether or not you feel the need to explore your energetic stance, it would be advantageous to your overall health and growth to enlist any assistance to locate and clear obstructions that you may not be fully aware of, and this can be of great help to your overall growth and well being. Do call upon me for guidance in this exploration if you are not currently engaged in this healing process, so as to allow your future to be one of longevity and happiness and good health and So It Is.

43

Love Is The Answer

LET US BEGIN A NEW DAY, a new day of joy and peace in the knowing that All Is Well. For it is seen with eyes of clarity and translucent light, focused upon the hearts and souls of all beings here upon the earthly realm. Do be advised to cleanse your perception from past angst and sorrow, and step into the day as though you are a new born babe without any preconceived ideas of what is to unfold, and allow the grace of all divinity to dawn upon your experience as you travel throughout your day.

Dear Ones, be advised to listen only to your own heart when in doubt or fear, for then you shall realign with Creator's Truth in being a vehicle of divine truth. For you shall exist without dualistic perception and see the world as it truly is. Now we see that your earthly experience is simply one of loving compassion for all, as you encounter various situations and relationships of communication among those you meet. For it is not what is said that is most important, but what love is exchanged energetically with everyone you meet. And you may wonder if everyone is deserving of your love and the answer is yes, of course, as all you meet within your sphere of being is truly those who gravitate into your field of existence. And you may be assured that giving love to all is indeed fulfilling your divine purpose.

Be it known that there are always those who may at times prove to be indifferent; however, this is not to be perceived as a personal reflection, in that they may be having a difficult day, and are not receptive to your loving stance. This is fine, for they will benefit from your caring love regardless of what appearances exist externally. Do not ever withhold your love, for it is infinite, and there is no amount that could ever deplete your source of love as you are a wellspring of joy, and know this is your truth.

As you move through your life, know that all the love you give and emanate out into the world is precious and more powerful than you can possibly imagine, for Thine is the Kingdom of Heaven upon the Earth and So It Is. It is written in ancient texts that those who give of themselves to others are blessed throughout all time and all existence.

Be aware that when someone is hostile or fearful or insecure, they are simply in need of loving acceptance. Yes, love is the cure for all that brings discord to one's being, and so know the beauty and power of your gift of love unconditionally to all you meet. There is no need to fear that you will be misunderstood, as love is pure and easily recognizable to all regardless of their personal stance. It is always the right way to converse, or to simply exist, so that the love of Creator flows through you unimpeded by judgments and reactive behaviors.

You see, Dear Ones, love is the answer. It has always been so and shall always be. For Thine is the Kingdom of Heaven upon this Blessed Earth and So It Is.

44

Always Trust That All Is Well

HERE AND NOW, Dear Ones, know that in the future there may be events of an unsettling nature and so you may wish to prepare, for these events are of their own karmic conclusion here upon the Earth plane. Do not be alarmed, Dear Ones, as these circumstances of karmic outplay are only a display of the fear and grief held within the hearts of those who still interact with the lower expression of dualistic behaviors. It is not for you to be concerned, only to send your healing love to areas of painful display, so that the residual effects of these events are assisted in healing.

Know that you are safe and free of the traumatizing experiences taking place upon the Earth, for those who suffer are simply expressing their imbalance in relationship to Creator's vast and immense Love for All. Even though there may be loved ones you are in relationship with who are confused and suffer these events in some form, know that this experience for them is one of their own choosing, so that they may find their way into the Truth of their own Heart. It is for them to make this choice, and it is also for them to conclude their experience here upon the Earth in the way they wish, so that they can continue their journey into the Heart of the One.

It may appear confusing to you, when you know love is the only answer that heals the troubled hearts of those who suffer. However, it is not for us to judge nor to alter, as they have unique paths leading to the heart of Creator's truth of their own making, and this is the freedom of free will choice. For those who choose to continue the dual existence of reality shall be allowed to do so, as they may need more development to understand the truth within their Being and Soul. It is not of significance nor evident of their worth, to continue along these lines of development, for they are embraced by loving Creator just as we all are. We ultimately are One and yet individualized aspects of being have the free will to choose what they need in order to become realized Beings of Light and Love.

Thus we find this time, although confusing to our perception, to be perfectly unfolding so that all may continue on their ever evolving quest to attain enlightened presence and freedom and loving wisdom. So do not dismay for All Is Well, and So It Is here upon the Earth as it is in Heaven.

Dear Ones, believe me when I speak that I do not wish to incite fear and worry within your hearts and minds, for what I see in the future is potentialities of what may occur, and nothing is set in stone, so to speak. Your continuing love and support for Mother Earth and all sentient beings can make a wonderful difference as to what unfolds in the years before us. It is wise to understand that All is Well, for this earthly experience is likened to a dream that is created through the individualized beliefs and unconscious programming brought about through eons of time, embedded within the genetic blueprints carried by all. Once the illusions created are dispelled, then one may see with clarity the truth of this illusive reality, and become free of its entanglement once and for all.

Be aware, that although some may choose to continue in dual reality, it is for their soul wish to do so. It is important to understand that although some may appear to be trapped in this illusion due to karmic expressions of suffering, it is entirely possible for anyone to break through this illusion at any point, if only they choose to do so. It is a choice of free will. So, Dear Ones, please know that all you witness external to your personal reality of loving presence, is simply the chosen experience of others so that they may grow and find their way into the Truth of their own Beings. Ours is to hold space for Loving Light and Compassion, for All Is Well.

45

The Creator Is Known
By Many Names

NEW TO THE PREMISE that all beings are One, is the idea that the Oneness of Creator's Presence envelops all existence throughout the Multiuniversal and Cosmic levels of Being. There is no more nor less, and this magnificence cannot be imagined by the mortal mind. It cannot be known within the context of mental or physical explanation, for the expansive nature of Creator's Being is in a continual state of flux and growth, and so it does not remain in a state of standstill at any point in your perception of time.

Indeed the Creator is everything and everywhere that exists as One Being of immense proportions that exceed your wildest imaginings. Dear Ones, the idea that we can discuss who and what the Creator Is, is in fact impossible, due to the realization that the Creator's entire being is indescribable in nature. For we as individualized beings can only experience a small portion of Creator's immense love, as we are individuated aspects that express various abilities and form and energy from a particular vantage point of consciousness within the Creator's Essence.

Thus, we can continue to grow and expand our perception of Creator's loving presence through our infinite exploration of multitudinous expressions of Creator's mind, consisting of light, love, sound, and intelligence that permeates all that Is throughout all dimensions of Being and beyond our perceived experience of what Is. Do know that you embody this light, love, sound, and intelligence to the extent that you are conscious of your own being and soul.

It is not required nor necessary to fully embrace the Creator's expansive existence, for only very few beings have evolved into a state of awareness that can hold the magnificent embodiment at the Cosmic level, which means they embrace greater amounts of Creator's Essence through conscious presence of responsible and perfect alignment to oversee the evolutionary development and expansion of these loving and creative manifest realities throughout the immensity of the Universe.

We know the Creator by many names, through various cultural belief systems that identify the essence of this creative energy existing as One Being manifest everywhere in everything. There exists nothing outside of this One and there exists everything within it, and so there is no separation, nor is there any illusive existence that does not contain this love, light, sound, and intelligence. Although some within your sphere of existence are in a state of disconnection from conscious awareness of their Truth in Being, they still are in a process of growth and expansion through the education they gather in their life experience. And so in a sense they are not separate from Creator's loving presence for they exist within this essence and can exist no where else.

For there is in truth no where else in existence other than within the body and mind of the Creator, and all individuated beings have the gift of free will choice so as to become conscious of their own alignment with their own truth in being. Thus, they become co-creators within the expansion of Creator's realm of existence. They develop into greater and greater awareness of the One of All That Is, through their own ability to experience how to allow the knowing and enlightened awareness of their soul expression in becoming fully manifest within their conscious experience. Thus all beings reach enlightenment, and awaken to their true nature to express their unique aspect in being a source of loving light and peace.

Know this, Dear Ones, that in keeping with your heart's alignment with the love of the Creator, you shall ascend into greater and greater heights of awakened presence, and thus manifest the Kingdom of Heaven upon the Earth and So It Is.

46

Now Is The Time To Live
Your Life In Truth

BEFORE THIS CURRENT REALITY of time and space within your dimensional expression of dualistic perception, there was once a time and space of living in peace and harmony upon the earthly plane. Knowing this is so is to know that this can manifest once again within the earth's experience in Being. It is not difficult to imagine Dear Ones, for within your hearts and minds you hold this vision, this knowing, that this is within the realm of possibility for your planetary consciousness.

To manifest this vision, it is necessary to act through the compassion you hold within your heart in all external matters that you encounter. Do not feel overwhelmed by this idea, for is this not your truth? Is this not your heart's desire? Know that what you envision within may easily manifest without. For you may experience peace and harmony in your lives at this very moment, without the need for the entire world to exist as you do.

You see, it is enough that your life is one of harmonious peace and joy to begin existing in the reality you are choosing, regardless of what chaos resides in your world. It is enough to simply realize, that through your cognitive decision to live your life now in peace and trust within the parameters that define your sphere of existence as a peaceful and loving space, where you encounter all as a reflection of your own personal projection in being. You see there is no reason to doubt that this can be, for you are the creator of your reality. And thus, you may live as you wish now, rather than sometime in the future when the entire world resides in peace.

Do realize, that although you find there are elements that affect your existence due to external outside influences, for the most part you may experience your own beautiful and fluid and peaceful existence. Never before has there been a time in the history of your planet where conflicting realities co-exist. Because of the evolutionary development of humankind taking place at this juncture, there are numerous avenues available to pursue within the loving stance you hold throughout your earthly journey.

Dear Ones, now available to you is the awareness that you need not wait for humanity as a whole to catch up to your stance in being. Living your life now in joy and trust, is not only possible, but is also in your best interest to step into the world you envision without further adieu. You see, for all the world's sorrow and pain, you may quicken the evolution of humankind through manifesting your personal experience as one of existing in peace. And this reality you generate shall begin to emanate and permeate the global collective consciousness, which will in turn bring the greater capacity for global peace to manifest.

Do not doubt this is so, for you shall continue your lives living as though the entire world has reached a pinnacle of achievement in it's evolution, and it is of no matter that this particular timeline does not reflect this in its material reality. For in time, your vision shall manifest through your ability to co-create a new plane of existence within the earthly dimension and It Is So.

Begin to live now, Dear Ones, as you wish to live within the Truth of your reality and your Soul. Now is not a time, but a vibrational expression of your inner presence, and may uplift and accelerate the vibrational range of the entire planet to also experience the Truth they hold within their Hearts and Souls. And So It Is.

47

Never Doubt The Truth Of Your Being

IT IS INDEED misfortunate for those who do not realize their own true worth, for everyone is an expression of Creator's grace and love. Those who appear lost, however, may not be judged, for they will in time become aware of their inner presence of love and light, and shine as brightly as you, Dear Ones, do now. And so do not despair for them, for they are on a perfect course of finding balance and alignment in Creator's Universe.

Some have karmic debts to fulfill, and in so doing shall realize the significance of their existence in the ways that best express who they are within their heart and soul. And so do know that even for those who suffer, salvation is at hand and they shall reside upon the planetary planes designated for their existence, so that they may fulfill their need to experience indifference and suffering in order to attain the perfect balance needed to align with their own Truth.

It is always a good idea to send those who are lost, those who are disconnected from their soul awareness, loving light with the intent that they awaken to greater knowing and presence of Creator's love. And this shall allow them merciful benefits in receiving the Grace of the Creator through many avenues of possibility. You see, my Dear Ones, it is not for us to decide what is best for another. It is for us to support others in love and exemplify right behavior and conduct in every situation. Thus they learn right behavior, and how this changes their perspective in living in a world of sometimes confusing situations borne of doubt and fear and resistant behaviors.

Always understand that we ascend at different junctures in our evolutionary development. It has always been so. Just as you embark upon your ascension journey now, millions upon millions of others have gone before, and just as you now embark upon your ascension journey millions upon millions of others shall follow, and It Is So. There is nothing to feel sorrowful about when viewed from this perspective.

It is a natural course of experience for all living within dualistic realities, and these particular realities exist throughout the Universe and beyond, as they develop through free will choice their liberation from dual existence. Thus, those who chose to misalign with Creator's essence will find eventually the balance they need to reunite with their true soul expression, and this is so as it has always been.

Not all beings choose to exist in dualistic circumstance. For they choose to exist always within the unique aspect they embody expressive of Creator's Essence, and these beings do not necessarily need, nor desire to experience lower vibrational dualism. Thus, they are free always, and to become liberated is not something that they experience for they were never not in a state of freedom. They have always chosen to experience the bliss and love of Creator in their existence. It is through their free will choice to remain in balance, just as you have chosen for various reasons to exist in dual vibratory exploration. For there is much to gain through this experience so that you attain an understanding and compassion for those who live lives of misaligned existence.

Thus, you have the knowledge of how this becomes a reality within Creator's Universe. Your compassion is borne of knowing and understanding the human condition upon your earthly plane. Even though you have endured much suffering in your lives, and have been indoctrinated into dual behaviors, you have found your alignment within the Truth of your Soul and so it is not to be considered a punishment, but a course of evolutionary development you have chosen, so that you may evolve in ways available through this system of educational dual based origin. Thus, you may journey onward with clarity and compassion that has developed through this experience, without which you would never know the depth of your compassion and understanding.

For I, Archangel Metatron, have experienced this reality myself many times, and due to this embodiment, I can fully understand the human condition within this circumstance, and can provide insight and help as to how to assist one to navigate through this dual experience in order to find alignment with their own Soul. And this is invaluable for my work as an Angelic Guide and Healing Presence in the Universe of the Creator. For the Creator is All and All exists within Creator's manifest realities. Dear Ones, know that All Is Well everywhere throughout all realities, within the Heart and Mind of Creator's manifest existence, throughout all time and all space, within and without, and So It Is.

48

To Exist In Peace Is To Exist In Love

PEACE OF MIND and peace of heart is of great significance in the years ahead, for now we must understand that this time of transitory revelation and upliftment is at hand. Which means, Dear Ones, that all are undergoing change for the better, regardless of what appears to be throughout the external circumstance. Dear Ones, it is essential that you release your angst and fears surrounding this transitional state, for this may hinder your ability to love and be loved, during a tumultuous period that may affect your state of mind and heart.

You see there can be no mistake when embodying the love of the Creator, for therein lies your power and salvation. To become the truth and love of who you truly are is essential, because it shall sustain you during the ensuing chaos around the globe. I do not wish to be a naysayer. Please understand my stance that I, Archangel Metatron hold, for I do not predict woe and grievous destruction. I simply foresee potentiality for the karmic energies playing out now and the direction they may be heading into in the future.

I do hope you can understand why I write this discourse, as it is my wish to prepare and sustain your stance of existing in a state of peace and love, regardless of what is to come. Do not fear and do not project worries of dark encroachment upon your lands of existence, for you are the creators of the new paradigm upon the Earth, and you shall live to experience a New Day dawning upon the world in Joy and Beauty and Peace.

Take heart in this knowing, and take heart in expressing compassionate love for those who suffer still. It is of divine orchestration that the future unfolds, dependent upon the openness of hearts to love and maintain peaceful countenance, in the face of what would be unsettling for those who do not possess the understanding of this karmic outplay of clearing and healing on a global scale.

Dear Ones, it is not for me, Archangel Metatron, to say what is to come and how your future unfolds. It is for me to support and protect and prepare you for whatever circumstance evolves in your world, so that you may maintain your heart center in love and peaceful coexistence with all the world's events now, and in the future. For in this is great power to promote and lovingly intend that the world be healed and transformed into a planet of peaceful harmonious existence. Through your ability to hold space for this transformation, is the key in assisting the Earth in her ascension process, and also for those whose hearts continue to open to the Truth of their Being.

Thus, there is great purpose and divine intention to overcome and to oversee this process of clearing and healing, so that all upon the planet may exist in a peaceful loving environment that respects and acknowledges the Sovereignty of All Beings, and, Dear Friends, this includes all Sentient Beings as well as humankind. And so do know there is truly nothing to fear, for all is well, Dear Ones. All Is Well. We seek the Kingdom of Heaven upon the Earth and So It Is.

49

Freedom Is To Align Through Free Will Choice

NOW WE SEE there are many questions arising within the hearts and minds of all Lightworkers who see much sorrow and confusion in the world, and they wonder why this is so, when the Creator could easily end this sad state of being globally through the ability to manifest peace and harmony in the world, by embracing everyone in discord with healing love. You wonder why such suffering is allowed in Creator's Universe.

I, Archangel Metatron, tell you it is so due to the nature of free will choice. Every Being upon the planet has the free will to choose what they wish to experience, and the Creator lovingly gives this gift of freedom to All. You see, Dear Ones, it is not for you to understand the suffering of others when it is not of your personal creation. It is for you to send loving compassion to those who suffer knowing this is of benefit to them, so as to influence their perception of truth, for they can receive, regardless of how much or little, your love, and your love is healing, and they shall know they are loved although it may not be perceived consciously. Still, they feel this healing love, and this can be of great importance in their lives, for heartfelt love is the key to opening to greater truth within their own hearts.

Know that even the smallest amount of love sent to someone or some area is received on some level of being, and this love shall eventually change the world to existing in planetary peace and harmony. Thus you are creating with your loving intent a new world, a new existence, borne of love and divine purpose. Even the smallest amount of loving intent has effect, and when you gather in groups for the purpose of sending healing love, the effect is exponential, and so do join in purpose with others of like intent to heal the world and all sentient beings upon and within this earthly plane.

Always, there is the need for love as this is the entire purpose of existing, so that all beings become aligned with their inner divine essence, so they may enjoy and serve and exist in loving coexistence, where all are residing within the conscious awareness of being multitudinous aspects of expression of the One Being Of Light, and this Being is the Creator of All That Is.

Know that I, Archangel Metatron, shall guide you in your pursuit to uplift the world and all its inhabitants, so that this vision of peace and love is manifest fully upon your planet. Be it known to you All, that I shall assist you in all ways possible when you ask for my help in any matter, regardless of how great or small, for all concerns you may hold require resolution. And I do ordain you to be fulfilled, so that all your cares and worries are dissolved in the Light of Truth and Love and inner accordance with the energetic flow of Creator's Divine Essence. Everyone who reads this discourse is Blessed and under the loving wing of I, Archangel Metatron. Know this is so and So It Is.

50

Living In Peace Is To Live In Love

NOW AND FOR ALWAYS know This Is So. To be upon the Earthly plane is to be where you have chosen to be, for you have enrolled in the school of earthly duality now and in the past. You have explored the dualistic domain of reality, and have succeeded in graduating into an understanding of what happens when one is not in alignment with Creator's Divine Essence. It is possible to stray from the truth of who you are, and this you know very well, for you have traversed through lifetimes of various incarnations that have been instrumental in allowing you to experience what dualistic systems of behavior create when out of balance with Divine flow. And so now you choose to become your truth, and now you choose to align fully with your soul evolutionary growth, and now you choose to ascend with your beloved Mother Earth and So It Is.

Your numerous lifetimes have not only prepared you for this time of transitory Ascension, they have also prepared you with the desire to assist all other beings to transcend this plane as well. And so this is a time to rejoice, Dear Ones. This is a time to express great gratitude and wondrous joy, for what lies ahead is a path carved in gold, so to speak. A path that leads to great illumination and enlightened presence among those of great heart, who have traversed these dimensional transitory realms before you, who wait with open hearts to unify their existence with you in full awareness of the Oneness of All That Is.

Do understand that now is a time to celebrate and to applaud the effort and accomplishment of those who follow their heart's desire to ascend with full recognition of where they are going and who they are, and this, my friends, is your destined point of arrival, so as to continue your journey with complete confidence and complete peace in being. For you now exist as Beings of Light unified with all creation in the multiuniversal domain of existence.

Seeing the beauty of your own lives within the context of future growth, along with so many other beings is remarkable and wondrous, in that you have helped to accelerate and to awaken many who now accompany you who may not have ascended at this time. Your work is invaluable and forever acknowledged, as tribulations of your world unfold, you are the salvation for many, as the Beacons of Light that you are have made a remarkable difference in the world. To continue your work of emanating love and peaceful demeanor out into the world, and in the presence of everyone you encounter in your daily lives, shall continue to make a remarkable difference in the lives of those whom you touch, and even the lives of those who are far from you receive the benefits of your loving intent to assist them.

You see, Dear Ones, your work is of immense importance at this time now more than ever. Your work is actually not work in that it is of a natural expression of the love that you embody, and so it flows with ease, and is like a river flowing unobstructed without effort or striving. You are expressing the healing love of Creator's Divine Essence, and this healing love is intelligent so as to emanate wisdom and truth and clarity to those whom you encounter, regardless of whether you exchange greetings and conversation, or simply walk past while holding space for your soul expression. For this is how immense the impact of your soul presence creates effortlessly and without necessarily your conscious intent. Simply being who you are is a gift to all and to all is the gift of your presence.

Your desire to help others within your heart is the essence of being a Lightworker, and so it is a natural state of being for you, Dear Ones. Do know that when you intend to send your love to assist others in whatever form you feel is called for, you are in fact uplifting the world as a whole and also all sentient beings within this planetary existence. Always know you hold the key to making this world a world of peace, a world of joy and love and abundant creation for All. And This Is So.

51

Blessings of Grace Ordained Upon This Day

TODAY OF ALL DAYS is the day you shall embark upon a higher understanding of what is meant when I speak of Truth Within. For truth within your own being and soul is nothing more, nor nothing less that your ability to perceive the truth of your own existence. To exist is to embody the Creator's manifest expression of Love. When one is in a stance of disconnect, they may not feel this love for they are entangled in lower vibrational energies of dual behaviors.

This dual existence is one of pain and suffering that has been created through the illusion that one is separate from the Oneness of All That Is. This illusion is created through the beliefs that we are separate from one another and cannot come into a place of unity within. This inability to connect into this truth in being creates dual behavioral systems, and so it is not known within the hearts and minds of those who are separated through their belief structures.

Be this as it may, there are other considerations that prevent one from embodying their truth in being, and those considerations are the inability to perceive life with the clarity of pure mind and pure heart. Thus, the inner presence of truth is difficult to express when one is in a state of misdirected focus in their perception in living. You see, Dear Ones, we cannot pursue a planetary shift of peace without this connectivity, and so it is impossible for one to exist within the higher dimensional states when one is out of alignment with the energetic flow of Creator's Love.

This being said, I, Archangel Metatron, shall invoke for All Humanity and All Sentient Beings, within and upon the planet, Blessings of Awakening and Joy for All. On this day and at this time, and hereafter evermore, All in existence shall rise into the Ascension of Creator's Being and All Is Forgiven for All Is Well. In this, I intend that all Beings receive the Grace of Creator's Love within, so that they, in their own time, through their own choices, shall eventually ascend into the Heavens of higher dimensional existence.

Prior to this blessing all beings were in route to the Creator's Heart through their own process, and so now I, Archangel Metatron, shall accelerate this process through the Grace of the Creator Ordained Upon This Day, so that more beings will ascend with Mother Earth, and those choosing a different route shall also receive increased Grace and Love for their evolutionary journey and So It Is.

This Grace becomes manifest through the upliftment of all beings who have suffered long and are entrapped in programmed manifest existence, without knowledge that they are indeed entrapped. And so this Grace shall open their minds in a new way, so as to perceive with clarity the truth of their existence.

In due time, they shall see with renewed eyes, and love with renewed hearts, so that their past karmic programs are erased and healed, releasing them from living countless lifetimes trapped within their genetic and physical karmic obstructions to their development, so they may move forward in their process with greater ease and greater clarity.

This I Say Upon This Day and Do Ordain This Grace to enter into the lowest of all physical and energetic domains in Being and So It is.

52

Freedom FromSeparation Is To Know Unity

FOR ALWAYS AND FOREVER do know, Dear Ones, that you are never alone in your journey into the infinite Universe of Loving Light. For you are indeed the essence of all that is, and you can never be separated from the truth that exists within the Oneness of All That Is. And yes, I do remind you of this often, and it cannot be emphasized enough, that you are all One in the presence of the Creator, and although there is sometimes interference in your perception due to illusive circumstance, it is always true regardless of your perception.

Believing that you are One is not the same as experiencing your oneness with all that is. To experience this unity, is to experience your truth in being so that all illusion falls away, and you know the freedom to exist as, and within the presence of divine love. To explain more clearly what this means is to say that you are simply Light, Dear Ones, connected eternally into the One Being that is the Creator. And to experience this reality requires that you relinquish all illusion that you are separate from anyone or anything, so that you encounter the reality of love that resides within the hearts of all, regardless of their stance and projected countenance.

You can never separate from Creator's Love nor can anyone else, for to exist, is to be an expression of Creator's loving intelligence and grace, regardless of how someone behaves. Whether they embody this awareness or not, is not the focus here. What is to be known is that all beings in all forms are manifest through the Loving Grace of Creator's Presence. So there is always this light within everyone and everything, for nothing exists that does not express the consciousness of the Creator.

All inert material seemingly exists in various states of expression. Even a tree trunk that has lost its form of soul expression, still exists as a remnant of Creator's presence manifest in physical reality, and so do not feel there is anything that can be separate in existence from the presence of Creator. It is easy to recognize a rainbow as an expression of the Creator. However, it is not considered to be as such when you look at discarded rubbish, for this is not lovely nor of a positive effect visually. However, the rubbish that has been discarded, was once created through purpose in being. No matter if its substance is inert or not, it is still formed by the substance existing in this life form of planetary origin, and so it cannot be separate, although its presence has deteriorated from it's original form and purpose.

For those living upon the Earth utilize the resources here, so that they may create forms that serve and amuse them and assist them in living lives of convenience and comfort. The manifestation of divine essence in physical form is truly magnificent, and so it allows one to experience creative manipulation in utilizing elemental substance. This expression is one of awe and wonder; however, it is mistakenly seen as something outside one's personal existence in that the form is different from other forms. And so the illusion is created that form creates separation, when in fact it is simply an extension of one's being born of intelligent ideas reflected in the object created. This object serves to evolve one's experience in being and so it is not separate from the one who created it in essence you see.

Items such as blankets and containers for food and such are created from the elemental presence of materials manifest here within and upon the earthly plane, and so nothing more exists than before, as it has simply changed it's form and purpose in being, and so this is the way it has always been. Creations coming into existence, and then fading or deteriorating or disintegrating back into it formation of origin in being that of the earth, once again cycles into new creations. Thus, there is no beginning and there is no end to the earthly expression of oneness within divine presence.

You see, Dear Ones, even just upon this planet you see the interconnected reality manifest in form, and so you also see how this changes throughout time. This is a manifest micro expression of the immense universe that exists, along with parallel universes that have no end and no beginning. All exists within the Light of the Creator, and so you, my friends, are manifest of this Loving Light and to experience your Truth in Being is to know you are integral to the Essence of All That Is. What this feels like to experience is blissful, when all illusion of separation is gone. Without your personality constructs and your belief systems, what exists is the Truth of your Divine Essence that is not separate, but interconnected to All That Is and So It Is.

53

Never Doubt Your Power To Change The World

NEVER DOUBT, Dear Ones, your own abilities to make a difference in the world, for you have great power and love within your being, and so do not hesitate to send love throughout the day to those who are in need of assistance. There are many oppressed who would otherwise wake up to the truth within their beings, and so sending them your light, your love, is of immense importance, for they may receive enough of your love to throw off the shackles of imprisoned behavior that obstructs their divinity.

You see, there are many who sleep due to programmed systems of genetic construction, so that they see only the veil of illusion before them, and do not experience their dimensional existence and unity in being. Through sending your love they may open to greater perception in living, and so they have a greater opportunity to awaken beyond the veil of illusion. There are those who find life upon your planet to be constantly filled with sorrow and pain, and to those who suffer do send your love in the knowing of the difference this makes.

For to send love energetically through your conscious intent, when born of your heartfelt desire to make a difference in the world, does indeed do just that. Dear Ones of Light and Love, know this is so. For those who have open hearts shall benefit enormously, as they are seeking love and healing, and so this energy of loving intent shall permeate their beings and souls, altering their perception in a profound way so as to illuminate their existence. Yes, your love is that powerful and this is not to be of doubt.

Only those who are completely closed within their hearts to receive this blessing of caring grace may only receive a minute amount. And although they cling to their existence of suffering, a small amount will still benefit their growth, although it may go unseen in an external sense. For those who weep, there is solace within their hearts, for there they do exist in loving presence, and even if their minds obscure their perception of the truth of their reality, they still belong to the unity of All That Is, and so they remain a part of who you are within. Healing your own self and sending healing love to others uplift the whole, and so know that your work is precious and helpful in ways you cannot possibly imagine.

I, Archangel Metatron, shall empower all loving intent to heal humanity and all sentient beings upon your planetary sphere. And so do know that when you send blessings of love, I also join in your intent to do so, and together we co-create a world that is harmonious and loving for all.

There are no other means to achieve a world of beauty and peace, for love is the answer as you all know, and love is the means to create a new world free of suffering and pain. This is to be so. Now and for always know that your work is what is changing all quality of life upon your planet, and know this is so in every thought, word, and deed you emanate within and without your existence in Being.

And So It Is.

54

Peace and Love Resolve All Conflict

PEACEFUL MEANS to resolve all conflictual energetic disruptions is always the way to amend discord, and so, Dear Ones, do remember to not engage in conflict when others around you are upset, or unfairly blaming, or expressing dire discontent. For when you react to the behavior of others around you with the same energetic response, then you are not only not helping them, you are lowering your own vibratory frequency to match theirs, and this is not good for you or anyone. And so do respond with understanding that they are expressing their discontent within their own being and soul, and it is not for you to experience their dramatic energy. For you can best assist another through maintaining and emanating your sense of peace and love, so as to allow them to rise to match your frequency.

This may be challenging at times when you feel unjustly burdened by the lower emotional turmoil someone else is experiencing, and they direct their discontent upon you, and it may feel unjust, unfair, unwarranted. However, be that as it may, it still does not benefit you to react in upset, for this pulls you down into their frequency in being in that moment, and creates difficulty in resolving the conflictual energies present. Through maintaining a loving and peaceful stance, one is able to effect the situation in the best way possible, and so it is important to have the inner strength to hold space for them to rise into the love and peace you emanate. It gives one direction as to how to deal with their feelings, rather than have them validated as real by reacting to them on their level.

You see, Dear Ones, it is for you to become a pillar of strength so that others may aspire, and release their stance to one of peaceful coexistence. It is never of any help to react in emotional frustration or anger, for it only exacerbates their condition of lower vibrational behavior. Only love can calm a situation when someone is misaligned in their stance. Only love can heal when one is feeling sorrow or anger or any other form of discord. For you see, it can only be for the best of all concerned to hold and embody the truth of your own being in every situation you may encounter throughout your daily existence.

Also, know that to indulge in idle chatter among friends who wish to discuss matters of lower vibrational frequencies of judgmental gossip, or conversations that condemn the actions of others, are also not aligned with the truth of your being however harmless they may seem. To indulge a neighbor's behavior of judgmental stance is to support this behavior, and it is not for their highest good to do so. Always know that when you reside within your heart, the words you speak have immense importance and effect, and so should you indulge in idle conversation that is misaligned with the loving presence of Creator's Essence, you are simply becoming misaligned also.

It is not for you to support behavior that reflects the lower dualistic behaviors upon this planet, and in not doing so it is actually easier to navigate conversational discourse when someone is not aligned with right speech. You simply smile and say what is in your heart, and what is in your heart is love. And so you are not conveying a response that is judgmental of them, but is simply the truth you feel within, and so they can resonate in that place, as it exists within their own selves. So you see, Dear Ones, you are able to communicate truthfully without personally being indifferent to their stance, for you are not in opposition, nor judgmental of who and what they profess. You simply express your truth and thus, they can respond without feeling subject to rejection of their ideas or words.

Therein lies the key to right speech, and when in right speech the other is uplifted to where you reside, rather than you simply going along with the conversation so as to not create hostility or discord. In this way, you may express your truth because you deliver your words with love, and this love energetically permeates your speech, and this creates a loving energetic space so that the other may join in your presence. However, if the person is not receptive, it is still in the best interest to hold a peaceful, loving stance. For then you at least are not entangled with lower vibrational behavior, and this is for your highest good also, even when another insists upon holding onto their angst or indifference. You see, Dear Ones, your inner truth shall guide you in situations of this sort, and you may continue to remain centered in your truth regardless of another's stance and So It Is.

55

Freedom From All Suffering Is For Those Who Choose To Ascend

EVEN THOUGH SOMETIMES you may wish that the world were already in a state of peace and harmony, it is alright that it is not, for the process your planet is undergoing is of immense transformation and growth, and this leads into the ultimate state your planet has desired to ascend into, so that she and all who wish to ascend with her shall experience a brilliant transition unlike that of any which has transpired before.

You see this process is unique, in that not only are you growing into a state of illumination, you are also ascending into Lightbody along with your planetary field surrounding the entire planet and all upon it. And so be assured that what is to come is the experience of a beautiful and peaceful and joyous existence here upon this marvelous planet, where there shall be no more suffering nor pain nor conflict nor fear nor dire need of anything. For this planet is destined at this point in time to be fulfilled in the intention to become a Being of Light and Love and So It Is.

Dear Ones, for those who choose to ascend after more experience within the third dimensional plane of existence, there will be Grace for them also in that they will be transported into a planetary system that shall provide them with what they so desire. However, it shall be an environment that enables them to progress with greater ease than what has transpired here before. For you see everyone is embraced in Creator's Loving Light and Presence, and because there is no separation, everyone is destined to ascend when they so choose.

Regardless of whether or not anyone wishes to ascend now or later, everyone shall experience liberation at the perfect time for their deliverance from lower vibrational behaviors, and so it is not to judge nor fear that anyone is being left behind. And so, Dear Ones, do not weep for those who depart and venture upon a different path, for all paths do indeed lead to the same place, and that place is total and complete loving presence within the Heart of the Creator.

You see there are so many paths which one may embark upon, and this is to be understood, for All are on a path now and will continue this journey into the Heart of the Creator. Now and again, I see you Lightworkers fall into despair and sorrow because you wish for everyone to become free of duality at this time and all at once. However, do not despair for it is the solemn gift from the Creator to allow each being the freedom to choose their own path of liberation, and so do take joy in knowing that All Is Well today and everyday. All Is Well.

The course Ascension takes is determined by each Soul Being, and they know what is needed to experience for their soul aspect to come into alignment with their inner truth. Dear Ones, this is so upon the Earth and any environment in which a being is experiencing third dimensional existence. There is no beginning nor end to the ascension process. As beings are born into individuated entities of the Creator's expression, they have numerous choices to experience existence, and they may also manifest throughout various levels in Being at once.

To choose to experience the reality of the material plane is available to them, and so when they become physically manifest in an externalized expression, they may choose to experience life in this realm free of karmic attachment. However, should they descend into the karmic realm of being due to various choices they make, they have the experience they have desired in order to become fully realized throughout all dimensions of Being, and this is of great assistance to their knowing of how Creator's Universe operates within these lower vibratory states.

And so with this knowledge gained, they may ascend into the higher levels of Creator's realms in being, while at the same time hold the knowledge of what transpires in the lower realms. This is advantageous for the depth of compassion attained within their Heart and Soul. And so you see, my friends, how this works and that All Is Well.

56

Know That All Is Well Regardless Of Discordant Events

THERE IS SO MUCH MORE to living than meets the eye of most people upon the Earth, for there is much transformational activity and purpose that the Earth enacts in being a supreme source of universal service. There is much that is not known to humanity in terms of what the Divine Presence of Mother Earth entails. She is more than simply a beautiful and magnificent Being, host to all sentient beings within and without her embodied expression of Divine Presence and Grace. You see, Dear Ones, your Mother Earth is a portal into higher dimensions of being and thus one may access greater dimensional embodiment through her various means of divine unfoldment. There are avenues that are not apparent to many because they are deluded in their understanding of the purpose of human existence.

Now we see many awakening to the greater possibility of living expressive of dimensional awareness in being. So it is in joy we receive your conscious connection into the higher realms of existence, while embodying your earthly expression of physicality. You are entering a realm where you no longer are entangled with dual behaviors, and will be able to manifest your true divinity without hindrance to your perception of truth and love. Thus, you shall reside upon the earth in a state of harmonious being and loving stance. This is in and of itself the creation of the new paradigm on this planetary journey into the Heart of the Creator.

Now is the time to engage in the expression of your divine attributes in your daily lives, so that you may emanate your truth and love for all that is. You are no longer hindered by lower vibrational interference that disrupts your aligned presence of love and light. This is to be taken as a sign that All Is Well, now and in the future, regardless of what other events transpire still expressive of the dualistic system that is indeed diminishing in presence in your reality.

For there is no means to disrupt the process of Ascension, regardless of what appearances seem externally. The process of Ascension is well underway and there shall be no recourse, for this process is mandated through Creator's own volition, and All Will Be Free who choose to endeavor to align in all they do and say and express in loving intent. There is upon the horizon a field of promise and joy as you enter into the new paradigm of Loving Light and This Is So.

Now and again we feel disheartened by the external appearance of dire events taking place throughout the globe, and this is not to be feared for these events are not of your making nor of your personal choice to become embroiled in. You are creating lives of loving intent, and healing within all that encumbers your heart and soul. And so in this ascension process the potentialities of becoming again entangled in dual realities are almost nonexistent, and I say almost, as free will choice prevails. However, those who have chosen to ascend are true to their purpose of manifesting the love of the Creator in their thoughts, words, and deeds, and so there is no likelihood that your intent would change at this point of awareness.

Be that as it may, Dear Ones, there is still much work to do in service to those who are not yet awakened. And through your own desire to assist others in planetary Ascension you may daily offer your prayers and intentions to heal and uplift humanity through your various means of healing modalities, and/or simple askance of their liberation through divine intervention. For all who exist upon this planet are subject to healing love, and with their unconscious desire to achieve liberation, they are enabled to receive this Grace. Do know This Is So, as this is Ordained through Creator's Loving Grace and So It Is.

57

Peace In Knowing All Is Well

NEVER HAVE WE ENCOMPASSED such great light and liberty upon the Earth, for the Earth is ready within the wholeness of her Being to ascend into the realms of higher dimensional existence, and this, of course, you may know. However, do you know that her ascension process is ordained to encompass all sentient beings upon her in her merciful stance of forgiveness for the eons of time where violent and aggressive behaviors have transpired? She has opened her heart and soul to encompass all the fields of dark influence surrounding and existing within the earthly dimension, and she is able to purify and transform these energetic limiting forms through her open and expansive Heart of Radiant Love and Truth.

You see, Dear Ones, the Earth is a Being of great fortitude and great courage, and knows no limits to her ability to love and heal, and so it is with great ease and trust that she envelopes the dark elements existing within the atmosphere surrounding your sphere of being so that her light permeates all darkness into the pure light of translucent loving transformation. Do know that her intent to heal and ascend with All is pure and true; however, she also, of course, allows the free choice of all upon her breast, and so in this light she ascends with those who freely choose her present course of travel into higher dimensional existence.

Although some will choose to journey into other spherical dimensions to experience their soul's growth as they so desire, this is well and good, for All Is Well throughout Creator's Universal Presence.

Do know that you will continue to meet challenges of different forms of expression, so that you continue to grow and align into the perfection of your being and soul. This can mean that some difficulties lie ahead; however, it is no longer necessary to suffer difficult circumstance when you are aware that All Is Well. Trusting that all is unfolding for your best and highest good will benefit your perspective of all that transpires in your life. For you hold the key to loving grace in that there is no experience that is not for your growth and expansion of awareness. And so it goes on and on and on and now you no longer need to feel confusion nor grief when challenging events occur. For you know within that All Is Well, and need not personally react through lower vibrational energetic response mechanisms, for you have risen into the awareness that All Is Well.

Dear Ones, do be diligent in your practices of meditative presence and increase this state of being through constant vigilant focus upon loving yourselves and loving one another so that you experience only love. For it is Love that will transform the world and transform your being into the Pure Light of Consciousness and So It Is.

Recent events foretell that much turmoil and sorrowful events are upon the horizon should they continue along their current energetic stream of unfoldment. And so, Dear Ones, always remember All Is Well regardless of external appearance. And I realize I tell you this once more so as to permeate your conscious awareness of this Truth, so you may navigate the woes of this world with ease and Trust that All Is Well.

Recently there have been enormous changes in the doctrines governing your planetary experience borne of dark influence, and let us say, this is their last hurrah for the dark elements existing upon your precious planetary jewel of light. For she is ascending and must transform all discord within her field of Being, and so she will move into higher and higher frequencies that will no longer allow dual behavioral systems to be present. And so she shall no longer support the energetic existence of lower consciousness life forms, as she has served humanity to the extent she can endure, and now must rise into dimensional planes of loving light so that she survives, along with those who choose to ascend with her.

She loves as much those who choose a different path; however, she must now let go of all that impedes her ascension process. Know that there is no being upon the planet that will not ascend in due time and experience; however, for now the Earth is leaving behind dualistic conflictual expressions of dire pain and suffering, and she is to be free in the realms of Divine Grace and So It Is.

Dear Ones, weep not for those who choose a different path, for those who do shall rise again to ascend in Grace also, just as multitudes have done before you, yourselves. There is no race to enter into the higher realms of being. All is well for One and All, as there is no separation nor lack of love, as every being is an expression of Creator's Divine Essence, and so do know that All will continue their journeys regardless of the path they choose. And So It Is.

58

Love Is All There Is

EVERY MOMENT there are forces at work to uplift humanity and all the world's inhabitants. For Divine Intervention has bestowed great volumes of light and love permeating the entire planet and all within and upon her as the Earth has clearly begun her Ascension into higher realms of Being. And so it is known on this day, that all Lightworkers who join in purpose to heal yourselves and others, shall be ordained to ascend along with Mother Earth. There are no other means to ascend than through the loving heart that transcends all lower vibrational expressions of dual behavior.

You see, Dear Ones, happiness and joy in being arrives when one realizes that All Is Well, and there is no other recourse to arrive into this stance, than through the Sovereign Heart of the One of All That Is. And there is no other recourse, than through the thoughts, words, and deeds of the one who exists in harmony with the divine unfoldment of Creator's expression here upon the Earth and throughout the entire Universe.

Every being upon the Earth is endowed with the ability to receive Creator's light and healing love, and so it is only a matter that one is open to receiving. Thus, you transform much the same as a flower blooms when exposed to light. It is without effort, you see, as it is as natural for you to ascend as it is for a butterfly to emerge from its cocoon. The butterfly does not try to become a butterfly. A butterfly simply allows its natural process to unfold without interference from outside disturbance, and so it is the same for you, Dear Ones. To naturally grow and flower within is to not allow others or certain events of dire conflict or pain to disrupt your trust in the beauty of Creator's unfolding nature.

There are many who are not entirely open to receive this light; however, even a small amount does have a tremendous impact. Thus, do send your brilliant light out into the world daily so as to maximize the number of beings to awaken at this juncture. And this is a blessing, as you serve the Creator through your own embodiment of love emanating out to everyone you encounter, regardless of what interaction takes place or not. For love is a force that permeates All, and when you simply receive the love of Creator within your own being, you also are sending this love out, as you physically embody this Grace in the physical dimension of Being.

In doing so you anchor this energetic connection into the earthly plane. Thus, all of humanity is uplifted as you vibrate these higher frequencies within this plane, and so all benefit from your embodied love through the collective mind of humanity. And all beings receive greater receptivity to higher vibrational thoughts and behaviors through your simply being the truth of who you are, and so your work is great upon the Earth and throughout the Universe. For all beings are empowered to become a greater force of love, regardless of where they may reside throughout the universal expression of Grace, and this is so, due to the nature of unity throughout the Universe.

When one embodies love more and more and more ad infinitum, then more and more and more beings are uplifted throughout the conscious mind of the Creator, which is everything everywhere in existence. And so, Dear Ones, your love for humanity and all on Earth shall emit frequencies out, not only into your earthly dimension, but also into the entirety of Universal Consciousness. For All is One, is it not? And so there can be no separation from the effect you create in emanating healing love. This love permeates and expands and moves continuously everywhere within the conscious mind of the Creator throughout all eternity.

Your love is like an ocean wave flowing out into the endless sea of Creator's Divine Essence, and it continues to move and expand its reach on and on and on, healing all discord that may reside within various areas of misaligned existence. As beings continue their personal growth into the vast expanse of Creator's Love, this loving wave contributes a great deal to the overall upliftment and healing of the Universe in its entirety. There is no beginning nor end to the loving expression of Creator's Presence throughout all Eternity. Love Is All There Is, Dear Ones, and so do live this expression of truth within your own beings for all separation is illusion, and you, in truth, are the Grace within the Heart and Mind of the Creator and So It Is.

59

Those Who Follow In Your Footsteps Do So With Ease

VARIOUS MEANS to elaborate upon that, which has been previously spoken, shall occasionally enter into future discourses in this book. However, do know that your understanding of the content of what is said can deepen and expand and so I, Archangel Metatron, shall continue to elaborate and repeat certain ideas so that you, Dear Ones, attain a fully and richer awareness of what wisdom is shared here. Only through your intent to receive this information, will there be development of your conscious awareness so that you shall expand and gain greater clarity and knowing of the Truth that exists within and without your Being.

You see, Dear Ones, only through the conscious intent to open to receive the words here may I implement a deeper awareness, so you will evolve and grow into heightened consciousness of the truths I speak of to you. You may then understand on more levels of your being what transpires in this planetary plane of existence in order to fully realize the truth of this reality that is hidden, so to speak, from mass access, due to traumatized experience programmed into the genetic linages throughout the globe.

Thus, this programmed information inhibits, and obscures the truth from those indoctrinated through cultural influence everywhere upon the Earth. For you see, there is no truth in the experience of dual behaviors, as the conflictual energetic exchanges are illusive in evading the true reality of being manifest in this physical expression of loving presence. It is with great sorrow that many continue to suffer when there is no need for such experience.

Although a large number of you, Dear Lightworkers, continue to emanate healing love flowing everywhere around the globe, there are still many beings who sleep in the folds of indoctrinated belief of fear and aggression. Only when one is open, may they receive the Grace that pours continuously into the furthest reaches of your environment. And when this is received in time (from your perspective) with the clarity gained, the deprogramming of fear manipulation and control loses its grip upon those who no longer fall victim to this entanglement of dire suffering and discord.

Do be aware, that although many will not receive this Grace of wisdom and love and clarity in seeing what truly exists in this plane of consciousness, they still continue to evolve, in that they directly experience through their free will choice the illusions that create reflective pain in being misaligned with their true purpose of embodying Creator's Love and Light. When they eventually have experienced enough of this pointless traumatizing and painful behavior, they will choose to find their balance, and open to the grace that is always available to them, and thus, find their alignment with the Oneness of All That Is.

Basically, when one does open somewhat to a new way of seeing, to a new possibility in existing, they can embark on a new avenue of growth leading to higher and higher states of conscious living, rather than once again looping around to experience more conflictual exchanges. And so it is possible for many many more beings to awaken into the expression of their heart's purpose and divinity. Peaceful coexistence among all beings upon the Earth is undoubtedly possible, and not only possible, but indeed ordained to manifest when all upon the Earth have awakened into their true reality, and this is not as far away as you may think, Dear Ones.

For this planet is on course for Ascension, and this process accelerates daily. Have you not noticed? For those who ascend along with Mother Earth are to experience great joy and love in their planetary sphere of high dimensional conscious existence. So there is nothing required in order to attain this ascension other than the letting go of indoctrinated beliefs of fear within the heart and mind, so as to elevate one's ability to embody love and connectivity to the Unity of All That Is.

It is rather simple really to understand from my perspective, however, for those of you who may still feel degrees of varying conflictual entanglement on occasion, know that this self created circumstance shall diminish in time so that you experience greater amounts of peace and tranquility in being. And when you reside in a loving stance in every moment of everyday, you shall ascend into the greater presence of God's Love and Light. This is so for you, Dear Lightworkers, are on course to ascend as your heart's purpose is on track, and not obscured by illusive constructs of societal origin.

Be aware, that even those who chose to ascend at a later time wishing for more dual experience within an oppositional reality, shall have greater ease in awakening, due to the groundwork you have laid for them in carving a pathway to follow, where your own footsteps have traversed leading to higher dimensional consciousness. So there is no place where your journey ends and another begins. It is more accurate to envision a continual stream of movement where all living beings are traversing at once through an evolutionary pattern of unfoldment, growing and expanding into the embodiment of their Truth. Know that This Is So.

The path you have created will leave less distraction and less confusion for those who will follow, for your light and love is illuminating the way for all. And so there is no beginning nor end to this process of attaining enlightened growth. For enlightened knowing and embodiment of love has no end and no beginning. There are always higher and higher dimensions of enlightened experience upon the horizon for you and eventually everyone, embraced in Creator's Love.

Although living in this world at this time may appear confusing and distracting from the loving purpose of your being, do not despair, for love heals All and in time this shall be reflected in your external planetary experience. Peaceful living and peaceful coexistence are available to experience now in your lives. There is no need to wait, for indeed living your Truth in Being is what creates and perpetuates the new paradigm in living and So It Is.

60

Fear Not For All Is Perfectly Unfolding Regardless Of External Appearance

RECENT EVENTS upon your globe are simply the tip of the iceberg of what is appearing upon your horizon, and so do not become distraught, Dear Ones, as more and more events of this nature occur. For more karmic interactive activity will continue for some time into the future before the nature of your global experience finds balance in its external environment. Be not afraid for many more beings will perish in the wake of the destructive forces still upon the planet, and there will be much sorrow and grief as the multitudes of dark influence behave in delirious confusion and aggression.

Please know as once again I, Archangel Metatron, tell you that all is well, and if this seems a trite and frivolous statement, I suggest you review discourse number 6 entitled 'All Is Well,' for it is there explained as to what this statement entails and what must be understood in order to not fall into fear or grief at this turning of the tides, so to speak.

Peace may be maintained within your being and soul, and so do not hesitate to send your healing love to all who suffer the conflictual events unfolding on the Earth. For when you send love I, Archangel Metatron, shall also send love to wherever you direct your focus so as to empower your intention.

Do not be alarmed as the visual external imagery appearing through your news outlets are not to reflect the love and peace within your being and soul. What does reflect your internal stance of love and peace is the knowing that all is well in your personal lives. You are knowing that you are safe, and that this karmic outplay is not a reflection of your karmic stance, for you are in the flow of Creator's ascension unfoldment. While at the same time, others are going in a different direction that will lead them eventually into Creator's comic flow of Ascension; however, only after they have fulfilled their desire to experience dual existence. And so it is not for you to weep, but to understand that all is well.

Do not be thrown by the tides of change and turmoil as there is much joy to experience in your ascension process, and there is much love to share with those who are not currently in flow with the Earth's Ascension. So, Dear Ones, I say to you once again, All Is Well. Be not distracted from the creation of your beautiful new paradigm that holds the promise of peaceful coexistence, and it is not for you to discern who shall ascend nor who shall leave the planet.

For some who are ascending are leaving physicality so as to assist in the Earth's Ascension from within the inner planes, and so this is to be celebrated in that they are fulfilling their heartfelt desire to serve in this process from within the higher dimensional planes of existence, while others choose to remain physically on the Earth so as to anchor the light and healing energies being showered upon this plane of existence. Do know that there is great work to accomplish as Lightworkers, now and in the near future, so as to anchor the magnificent and merciful healing power of the Creator so that many more beings may awaken, and so that many more beings may heal and arrive into the truth of their own being as they begin to see more clearly the truth of all existence.

Thus, there is great joy in this transmission of light frequency codes being delivered into the heart of Mother Earth emanating out through all sentient beings existing currently upon the Earth. And so, Dear Ones, it is not for you to judge what is happening before your eyes. It is for you to know that all is well, and to trust the karmic balancing taking place. Do not fear and do not grieve, for All Is Well within and without.

Do trust your own ability to understand the premise of karmic acts bringing balance in mysterious unknown ways to your perception. This is not to say that pain and suffering are a desirable means to transition from the Earth. However, it is up to each individual soul aspect to choose their experience in leaving the earth plane now or in the future, for they are on their soul journey of evolutionary experience and So It Is.

Now be aware that when you journey to other areas, that you are clear in following your guidance in terms of timing and location so that you may traverse the land without fear of encountering interference from the energetic turmoil present upon the earthly plane. To listen to your heart is essential during these times of uncertainty. And to listen to your inner guidance as to what feels easy and right, is to navigate with ease and trust that you shall be moving in resonance with the ascension process. There is no need to take shelter nor stay in one place during this ensuing transition.

Indeed some will be called to travel to new areas so as to anchor the light where it is most needed. This is not to say that you would locate to areas of dark influence or discordant communities; however, it does mean that it will be possible to travel elsewhere as you feel guided, and to enjoy this travel, and enjoy a new place to reside that carries the vibration of enlightened Ascension.

Be it said that there are many paths to enlightened existence, and the roads are many and varied. Be assured that your personal paths are paved in gold and you shall receive the Blessings of Universal Protection and Grace in your ascension process, and so do not hesitate to travel if you so feel inclined, as living in the New Paradigm does not involve any form of fear and So It Is.

61

The Loving Heart Is All Powerful

ONCE AND FOR ALL, all Lightworkers may know that there are more and more factors to consider when sending their healing light into the world. It is imperative that you give your utmost to assist humanity and all sentient beings so that as many as possible ascend at this juncture. It is also imperative that you focus upon those who need the greatest assistance so that the Earth can come into a balanced state more rapidly. With your light and love much is to be gained when you direct your heart flow into those areas of greatest need, for this is where the discord is most prevalent and energetically out of balance.

You see there are numerous ways in which one may send loving light to illuminate the conditions of discordant suffering, without the need to become emotionally entangled with the circumstance. For you, Dear Ones, are of immense support and help to those who suffer the slings and arrows of misfortunate events, and it is for you to act in compassionate, loving response without the need to suffer these events along with those who do. For it is not for you to grieve nor become heart broken over the upcoming events, and so do not fear that all is not well, for you know at this time All Is Well regardless of external appearances.

What is seen externally is the dire results of dark interference with the beautiful and pristine nature of the

Earth. You see this influence has transpired numerous lifetimes of those now present upon the Earth, and it is not so readily transformed by those who carry much past and present lifetime sorrow and grief imprinted upon their DNA and within their heart and souls. For they do not realize that there is the opportunity to heal and release old patterns controlling their behavior. For some, this is unfortunate due to their lack of knowing of higher dimensional existence, as they are not aware of the Divine Grace available to them, and so they insist on seeing the world through eyes of indoctrinated beliefs, and thus, they are limited in what they perceive as possible.

So, Dear Ones, your loving light is magical in that it permeates this programming that controls the existence of many, who otherwise would be joining you in the ascension process now in motion. It is imperative that you give generously your light to those who sleep, for it is powerful beyond your knowing, and it is powerful in healing and opening the hearts of those you focus upon. It may not appear to be creating much change in the world; however, do know that it is making immense changes within the hearts and minds of those who receive your grace.

And yes I do say Your Grace, as the love that you emanate is indeed the Grace of the Creator, and with this grace comes a responsibility to dispense this infinite resource out into the world on a daily basis. Indeed it is possible to emanate this grace in every moment of your existence when you are residing within your Heart. Know This Is So. Know your every loving intent is manifest without hesitation, empowered through your own channel of grace that you embody. While at the same time your connectivity to the One of All that Is broadcasts that intent, and all Divine Beings who feel called to assist also empower your graceful intent. This happens of its own accord without the need to consciously ask for higher dimensional empowerment, and So It Is.

It is truly a wonderful and shared experience to give of your own heart, for in doing so you are also anchoring the powerful and compassionate love of Divine Beings in the higher realms of consciousness, who also contribute to your heartfelt intention. And this is how it works, Dear Ones. This is how mountains are moved through loving intent. Along with your heartfelt desire to heal, the immense love of the divine realms within the inner planes also empower your loving intent. Thus, mountains can be moved, so to speak, as the enormity of the powerful transmission of Grace is far reaching and permeable to where it is focused, and this is not to be misunderstood as a biblical reference. It is to exemplify the true power of healing love manifest upon the Earth when Lightworkers send out their Love. It is so easy and simple to do, Dear Ones, so do enjoy your ability to simply send love into all areas of discord and to all beings who suffer.

It is for you to know and to embody the Divine Grace of all beings in Unity of Purpose, in combining forces of healing love through your physical vessel's earthly presence to manifest into your earthly plane of being. And I do hope this is clear in your understanding, for you do not ever work alone when you reside within your heart and soulful purpose in being. It is always with the awareness that the Universe of Creator's Presence is essentially the true wholeness of your Being. Bringing light to areas of darkness is your divine purpose in being upon the Earth.

Recently there have been great strides in bringing greater awareness to the masses, and although your media outlets focus on the sorrows of the world, they would do well to report the immense and beautiful upliftment taking place. Amid all the chaos, is the renewed promise of living in peace and harmony. In due time these glimmers of hope will manifest more and more, and so do have faith in the love you hold, for it is powerful beyond your knowing and So It Is.

62

Always There Is To Be A Peaceful Stance Within In Creating The New Paradigm On Earth

PEACE IS NOT AN IDEA. Peace is a state of Being and so, Dear Ones, please know that within your heart there is much sorrow that is in need of releasing from your past incarnations and also from your current incarnation. So be it to say, that when you take a look at the world's troubled stance, it is disconcerting, to say the least; however, it is not for you to suffer any longer, for you are on the precipice of a new day dawning. This new day is a day of peaceful coexistence and loving interaction among all sentient beings, and in truth this is glorious, is it not? To exist without fear, without self doubt nor self recrimination is to exist in the truth of who you truly are, and who you truly are is the loving Divine Essence of the Creator. Seek only peace in your lives now and always, and live today as the new day dawning upon your planet, for in your own lives you create this new world. It is through your own hearts that divinity blossoms, and is expressed in every thought, word, and deed, as you embark upon the new paradigm of peaceful coexistence.

And how is one to do this when they are surrounded by terrible news everyday? It is not for you to suffer the transgressions of others who sleep and exist in the fearful construct they have adopted as their reality. And so it is necessary for those of you who still weep for the plight of others, to instill a new awareness that allows them to transcend the third dimensional plane of dual reality, and this is accomplished by simply living life as you desire it to be. So that when you wake in the morning, do not attune your mind nor heart to the horrendous exploits happening externally. Do attune your heart and mind to the frequency of peaceful loving existence, and allow yourself to experience joy in your lives.

Understand that to live in peace and joy does not mean that you are not aware of the suffering of the world. It simply means that you no longer exist within that field of expression. You exist in a field of loving compassion, and continue to grow and expand without the traumatized experience of dual behavioral systems. And so you may offer your love and joy into the world's current condition as you are Beings of Loving Light and are aware that many may benefit from your presence here upon the Earth.

Although there are those who choose to continue their perception of the world through eyes of dualistic programing, it is best to also hold them in your hearts and prayers, so that they may someday be capable of receiving the love being dispersed everywhere throughout the globe through the loving compassion of your hearts. It is possible that even those who appear the most disoriented may still eventually awaken for they are all within the loving embrace of Creator, and whence they receive even a minuet amount of healing love, they may expand upon this and grow and enliven their own hearts and souls so that they shall someday step fully into their Truth.

This is important and bears repeating my friends, for you will do well to remain mindful that your loving compassion is immensely powerful and of immense impact. And so do not delay in giving of your beautiful heart as you exist in the sphere of your new paradigm, without the grief and sorrow you may now feel for those who suffer. It is best to say that when you decide to embody this new world in thought, word, and deed, then it shall be so upon your earthly realm of being, and thence there shall be joy for all and freedom for all. For Thine is the Kingdom of Heaven upon the Earth and So it Is.

Do not hesitate to take joy in the beauty and loving relationship of community, as you are deserving of great happiness. And it is not wrong, nor inappropriate to feel great happiness while knowing of others who suffer. Indeed, through this joy you also exemplify what is appropriate in being, and in no way are you ignoring the plight of others who sleep, nor are you being uncaring for their condition. For in your hearts your joy and love permeate the environment surrounding you so that others may join in your expression of worldly peace and love.

For once there is harmony and loving relationship among all upon the earth, then shall peace reign throughout all the lands within the hearts of All Sentient Beings. And those who leave the planet to traverse other systems of experience shall also grow and evolve without the need to be programmed into dual realities, unless they so choose, as it would be of their own creation. In manifesting into a different system outside of dark influence, they have a fresh start so to speak, and shall experience free will to create their world from within a clearer perception. So do not weep for them, for they shall grow and be free in the time they choose. I do hope you are understanding of why all is well, Dear Ones, for All Is Well and It Is So.

63

Weep Not For Those Who Suffer For In Time All Shall Be Free

ALWAYS TIME and time again I shall say to you, Dear Lightworkers, all is well. For I see many of you who are broken hearted, and have allowed your emotionality to overwhelm you in the face of dire trauma upon the Earth, and I say again to you, All Is Well. For the forces of good and the forces of light are raining down upon your field of existence, and this means that all is being enlivened and healed and transformed so that all of humanity receives the Loving Grace of the Creator. It is not just for some and not others. It is for everyone and everything existing on Earth.

Do know that in the course of events it is said that 'all things come to pass' and this is so when eventually you open to the knowing that nothing goes unnoticed nor ignored. For even the smallest of creatures upon the soil of your existence receives the uplifting Grace of divine interventive forces, and so it is not for you to grieve, nor it is not for you to exist in sorrow for this dims your light, and your Light is the Truth of Who You Are Dear Ones. It is the alpha and the omega of your vibratory existence, and I do not say this lightly. I say this with the full intent of the dynamic voice of the Creator's Truth in All Things.

Do not hesitate to call upon me, Archangel Metatron, for I am with you whenever you ask for my assistance in any matter great or small. I respond through your heart generated intent that connects into the Oneness of All That Is, and I hear you, Dear Ones, loud and clear so that I may assist you in all ways possible for your best and highest good. If you trust this is so, then it shall be so.

My Dear Lightworkers, you sometimes feel weary and sometimes feel discouraged as you do not see the changes you wish for occurring. However, do know that much is occurring in the way of transformation, so that there is much to celebrate among one another and among all beings upon the Earth. Peace and love shall be the norm for all earthly life for those who choose Ascension. For you see there are many who are awakening, and there are many whose hearts are opening as never before, and it is because of the light you are emanating out into the world, Dear Ones. It is because of your devotion and intent to heal the world.

I cannot begin to describe the wonderful changes occurring within and without your global existence. Do trust this is so and so it is. For now more than ever, light is permeating the hearts and minds of those who may appear to be lackluster in nature, for even those who sleep embedded in old patterns they hold onto, even for those beings who are not receptive to opening their eyes and hearts, are receiving Grace from the Divine Beings emanating from the inner and outer planes.

Recently there has been much sorrow reported through your news outlets and there shall be more to endure. It is with great sorrow we on the inner planes experience the dire violations of humanity; however, we foresee a time of great joy for all. And our expression of sorrow is not to be misunderstood, for we do continually hold great love and light for even those who create these misdeeds, for they know not what they do. Having this been said, your news outlets do not describe the brilliant transformative energetic impact your light is creating for all of humanity and the entire world.

For now it is crucial that you continue your healing work and your trust that all is well, for All Is Well and all is evolving and healing and transforming into higher dimensional existence for All. Those who still sleep may or may not awaken prior to the Earth's Ascension, and it shall be perfect in and of itself. So that those who choose to experience living in a new paradigm shall, and those who choose to exist in an environment of dual behavior shall, however, without the dark influence that encumbers and restricts their perception of truth.

It is for you to realize that all is well not just in thought but in reality, for all sentient beings upon the Earth shall be free, shall be liberated in the time they so choose. For now the dark influence is being swept away through the immense light and love permeating the entire sphere of your existence and all is well. There is no need to weep, for you are free, Dear Ones. You've only to realize it and to trust that All Is Well and So It Is.

Eventide of future events shall not dissuade your perception that all is well, for you understand that free will choice is playing out in the dramas unfolding before your eyes, and this is not for you to suffer. It is for you to live in peace and joy so as to bring the new paradigm into your reality. I assure you again and again and I shall continue to assure you, All Is Well upon the Earth as it is in Heaven and So It Is.

64

To Live Naturally Is
To Live Freely

EVERY TIME YOU SEE a rainbow you marvel at its magical quality of light and color, and so it is revealed to you the etheric presence of God in a simple form. You wonder how this may manifest in your life, as though it may be a positive sign that all is well with you, and perhaps the world. This is so, Dear Ones. This Is So. For the magic you perceive is indeed an example of the promise of the Creators Grace.

Every time you perceive a magnificent sunset you marvel at its beauty, and you are for a moment, enraptured in its essence and so you feel great awe for the wonder you are witnessing. Every time you see a baby, you marvel at its perfection and innocence, and you delight in its presence for it is a bundle of joy before your eyes. Every time you experience the feeling of water around your body, you take pleasure in the liquid magic surrounding you, and so you feel relaxed and embraced as though you were being hugged with loving arms. Every time you sense a fragrance of sweet floral origin, you take a fuller breath so that you may embody this wondrous essence, and you enjoy the effects of this sweetness drawn into your being. Every time you see a mountain, you marvel at its omnipotence and majesty, for it is overwhelmingly present beyond your reach. Every time you make a wish, you hope it will come true, for you somewhere within, believe you deserve to have this wish manifest and so you believe that it can be so.

Dear Ones, these sensations demonstrate the wonders you encounter everyday, and it is magical indeed that you respond so naturally to these occurrences, for you are indeed beings of nature and integral to the life of your planetary existence. So you see it is not unusual to encounter magic on a daily basis through the experience of simple and beautiful expressions of natural origin. It is not unusual to experience within your daily life the wonders of creation, and so do know that this is true for everyone, even for those who do not consciously respond to what they consider to be ordinary or mundane. It is still enjoyable for all to experience their natural environment, and so it is also natural for everyone to feel an affinity for beauty and joy, and this, my Dear Friends, is my point.

No matter who you are nor how you perceive the world, everyone can experience the beauty of creation, and this beauty is also existing within themselves, as we are all manifest of natural origin. It is best understood by those who have hearts of loving acceptance, that the beauty within our very souls are reflected in this pristine and beautiful planet know as Mother Earth.

It is not surprising then that many beings who sleep have opportunities to awaken simply through the magnificent display of magic surrounding them. You see, Dear Ones, the Earth herself, is expressing much grace through the magnificence of her soul expression. For as she is within, she expresses without, and as we are within, we express without. In focusing upon the all pervading beauty of the world, we begin to heal ourselves within, and So It Is.

To focus on what is not of natural origin, such as waste and trash and disorder of natural elemental design, will confuse the soul and disturb our equilibrium. Thus we feel out of place, rather than comfortable in our natural environment. You see it's not so much about what exists, as what you focus upon, and to focus upon what magic exists within your reality will manifest more and more magic in your lives. This I do say so as to encourage all of you to direct your mental focus upon the higher expressions of your natural world. When you reside beside a river there is a wondrous experience of peace coinciding with the ceaseless movement of water flowing. This place is one that nurtures your wellbeing and mental focus. When you reside in an area of discordant sounds and energies, such as your cities that have deteriorated in quality of life, you will feel much discord within yourself, for your experience is reflected within.

And so I say to you, Dear Ones, choose wisely your living environments, for they do make a remarkable difference. When you wish to exist in peace and harmony, an environment of natural sound and rhythms are most beneficial to your health and wellbeing and also to your spiritual growth. It is draining and confusing to live in circumstances that are out of sync with natural rhythms. It is also not healthy mentally nor emotionally. This is not to say that living in a city is detrimental in general. It is to say that living in various areas within a city that carry lower vibratory energies can be detrimental to one's wellbeing.

Do understand that where you reside and the quality of the people in your community do affect your overall wellbeing and soul. For even those whom you love sometimes may not be of beneficial influence on you, and this is not to say to avoid the presence of good people who are not aligned with your process. It is to say, those whom you spend the most time with in community will support and understand who you are, and how you live your life so as to encourage your focus and heartfelt intent to evolve and expand in ability and growth. Many of you may already reside in areas which are supportive in this way. However, if you find yourself in an area not resonate with your energetic stance as a Lightworker, then you may wish to relocate to where you may find community of like mind.

Now this being all said, do know that wherever you live, so long as you live within your heart and soul in expressing your utmost in the world, it is precious that you are here lending your helping hands and heart. You are greatly appreciated and supported on the inner planes, and you are never alone regardless of where you reside. Although you may wish to enter into a community of loving Lightworkers, it is all right if you reside in a circumstance where you feel somewhat isolated, for in Truth you are not. When you reside within your heartfelt purpose in Being you are residing within the Grace of Creator's Loving Embrace. Do know that you may call upon me, Archangel Metatron, for any guidance you may require. And So It Is.

65

Freedom To Live In Peace Is Now

DEAR ONES, and I say Dear, for you are precious in my eyes and in my heart. For all the world benefits from your presence within the earthly plane, and so it is with great love I hold you in my Heart and Soul, for you exist in the Unity of All That Is. It is ever so dear, and ever so powerful to have your devotion in service to all humanity and indeed all sentient beings in the land in which you reside. It is for you to know that this service is greatly valued and shall be rewarded with the glory of heavenly entrance into the higher dimensions of Being.

Dear Ones, again I say to you, do not fear the coming changes, nor do not grieve the losses of those who have chosen to leave your planet at this time, for all is well. All divine beings are Blessed and shall reside along with you in the heavenly realms of ascending consciousness. It is to be known by you all, that peace shall reign on Earth as it does in Heaven. For, Dear Ones, beyond the veils of illusion, lies the Truth within your Beings, and all of Creator's Universal Presence manifest in millions upon millions of life forms that reside with you in Unity of All That Is.

I speak to you of this, as now you are ready to ascend into the ever flowing light of God's Grace so that only goodness and love become your daily reality, even though it does not appear to be always so within the events you witness outside in the world. It is for you to live your joy and peace in this moment and here forever after. For it is ordained upon this day, that all beings great and small, shall arrive at the gates of the heavenly portal, if not in this current cycle of upliftment, then it shall be so in future cycles for those who choose to take a different path of Ascension. All shall rise into the bliss and joy of being within the truth of who they are, and so take solace in this knowing and live your lives freely without fear nor trepidation, as the Kingdom of Heaven is here upon the Earth as it exists within your minds and hearts and So It Is.

Peace becomes you.

Love becomes you.

Trust becomes you.

Love becomes you.

Light becomes you.

Love becomes you always and in all things.

Dear Ones, let this be your experience and let this become your reality and truth in residing here now upon the Earth. There is no need to wait to experience your joy and love in living.

Dear Beings of Light upon the Earth, please know that I, Archangel Metatron, and a host of multitudinous Beings of Divine Grace focus our assistance upon your every need so that you are fulfilled in your quest to ascend and evolve in this cyclic period of ascending grace. For you are ready, Dear Ones, to relinquish all holds of lower vibrational dimensional illusions, that in the past have held you in check so that you were lost in delusional existence of conflict and dire suffering. Now you seek the Kingdom of Heaven, and now you receive with open hearts and minds the loving Grace of Creator as you awaken into the Truth of your Beings.

It is for some to continue their journeys in dual systems of oppositional stance so as to further their development of conscious alignment, and this is well and good for their souls know what they need in order to ascend and experience divine growth. It is for you to let go and to relinquish all ties to everyone, so that All are free to pursue their personal path of development.

This is not to say that you do not love them nor wish to assist them. This is to say, you are to not become entangled in their emotional turmoil as they experience their own personal growth through dire conflict, and this is for their wellbeing.

For they are to eventually align with the divine purpose in being you see, and so accept and allow them to have the freedom to choose their manifest reality.

As in time, from your perspective, they shall see through the veils of illusory obscuration, and be able to live in peace residing with you in the future to come. So they are not separating from you in truth. They are never separated from the unity of All That Is, and so no one can ever be lost and no one can ever be condemned forever to suffering due to lack of awareness. All in the eyes of Creator are redeemed when they open to the Grace of Loving Light that permeates the entire Universe and Beyond.

For the Creator has always been present in every particle of its entire Being and no one and no thing may ever separate from this Divine Essence. It is within all, and it is only through believing in the illusion of separation that a soul aspect comes into a stance of suffering, and this suffering is created through the illusions self created. These illusions are now falling away, and for those who see more clearly the truth of their reality in being, shall soon awaken and rise along with all those who have before them, and join in the One True Light of all existence. And so it is nonconsequential that some ascend sooner or later, for All shall through Creator's Grace in due time.

So do take joy in this knowing and accept the chosen experience of everyone in their journey into the Heart of the Creator where they all manifest from to experience their own Being in Truth and flow of the creative expression of vast and enormous ability to sojourn throughout the entire Universe and this is so, Dear Ones. This is so.

Do realize that when others look downtrodden or confused, your simple presence of love and compassion shall uplift their hearts without your even interacting, and if there is simple interaction then this shall be an even greater gift, as you emanate a high frequency of higher dimensional stance. So know that, without trying you make an immense difference, and through your lightwork, you lift up the entire world.

Your loving compassion is of great importance, as you are like a portal of higher dimensional Grace flowing through your Beings and Soul. And so know that you are essential to the creation of the new earthly domain of peace. Love envelops your every moment. Breathe it in and enjoy the peace of your existence today and everyday, for All is Well.

66

Always Be Present Within The Loving Heart

TODAY DO NOT FEEL surprised if I tell you that although there are many ways in which to heal and clear traumas from the Earth plane, the best and most efficient means to heal is through the simple love of your hearts. For you see the energetic flow of love sent out to all beings upon and within the earth is of enormous velocity and impact when you combine it with your intention to heal.

It is known that there are many methods of healing and all are wonderful; however, if they are enacted without love, then of what value does it hold really? It is not enough to practice a technique with intent to heal. It will not energetically connect to the great power of love unless you are truly feeling this love within your being and soul. Ah, that is where the magic of transformation is! To love the world and one another is simply the key to transforming the entire world into a land of peace.

Every moment do be in this stance of sending love from your being and soul and then quite quickly transformation occurs, for being the change you wish to see in the world is the way this transformation happens in and of itself. You see there are numerous avenues of healing and love is the driving force within all of them. So do not hesitate to open your heart and let it emanate anywhere and everywhere you are for it is contagious.

When a smile is given filled with loving intent, this simple act can awaken the love within another, and then that one emanates this love and so on and so forth.

You understand that you already embody love much of the time as it is; however, do you find times when you are hurried or feeling pressured to be somewhere or to do something? Yes, I see this is true for most, and this is understandable in the scheme of earthly dealings throughout your day. However, might I suggest you take a breath and center within your heart for just one second and then proceed with your demands of daily existence. It is to be known that others shall perhaps also take a moment to perceive your hearts presence and also embody their own, as your actions and gestures and energetic presence do emanate your love even if you are hurried or feeling the pressure of demands to be met.

It is not for me to give you direction when you already know this to be of importance in your daily lives, however, it is for me to remind you of the value of existing within your heart at times when you feel distracted by daily procedures requiring your attention. It is easy to become caught up in your work of a mundane nature, and so this does happen when your attention must be focused upon achieving what you must accomplish.

This being said, Dear Ones, the love you do emanate is of immense and beautiful effect upon the world and all beings within it. You already flow with tremendous love from your hearts and soul, and it will be even more powerful when you become conscious to exist in this state in every moment, for it is for your benefit to do so as well. You see there are numerous avenues of expressions of love, and this expression can be continual and a constant in your lives. So do intend to become more aware of when you become embroiled in tasks that love may still flow from your hearts. Thus, you embody greater love and presence of Creator's Divinity.

Always ask for me, Archangel Metatron, to prompt you when you are at a loss for what to do when you are entangled in a situation that distracts you from your loving heart, and I shall assist you in centering and refocusing your presence. Thus, you will find existing in your heart space to be helpful in resolving what has challenged you. Do be aware that when challenges arise, responding in love is the best possible solution, and yes, this is easier said than done, Dear Ones. However, it is worth the endeavor to do so, for you then will find the situation is resolved more readily.

Dearest Beings of Light upon the Earth, I, Archangel Metatron, do support you and cherish who you are as you bring the light into the lives of those who sleep, and in ever increasing numbers they are awakening. Do continue your work in healing those in pain and suffering, for they shall rise in the acceleration of the ascension process due to your undying love and compassion. This is the Grace of Creator realized through you, Dear Ones. This is the Grace within your hearts emanating out into the world.

Be it ever so humble there is no place like the Loving Heart. To live within a peaceful and loving countenance in your daily existence is to indeed transform the world. So simple, so profound, so healing to all you encounter is the love flowing within, connecting you to the mighty power of All That Is. May Peace reign within your Beings and may you find solace in the Love already present within your lives. And So It Is.

67

Daily Intend To Shine Love Into The Hearts Of All

REGULARLY I WOULD SPEAK of matters concerning your process and your beliefs regarding your lightwork; however, today let us speak of global concerns that are hindering the wellbeing of your planet. You see there are many many ways in which we may assist the Earth in healing from the imbalances brought about by humankind, through their unconscious creations of dire misaligned behaviors that hinder the wellbeing of humanity and the entire planet.

It is for us, the Divine Beings within the inner planes, and for those of you externalized into your dimensional stance on Earth, to develop greater and greater embodiment of love, for this indeed is what shall transform and heal the Earth. It may be difficult when you see others who do not exist in love to send them yours. However, you taking the initiative is essential so that they may awaken. For those who do not feel the love within their own hearts are deprived of the very essence of their own soul, and when you send them love, it can awaken their spirit and stimulate right behavior when they experience it exemplified in you.

For you see, Dear Ones, it is essential that you bring about change in humanity through your devotion to healing everything and everyone, and it is with no effort that you do this. It is simply through your ability to exist in love that is required in order to uplift the hearts of those around you, and it is quite natural for you to assume this stance throughout your day more and more and more as you embody your own Truth in Being. You see there are numerous avenues of communication that you may experience daily, and although they differ vastly, the thread that runs through all your discourse and interactions is love, Dear Ones, is Love.

However, there is more to say on this topic, and it concerns those who are ambivalent as to how they should respond to your love. They may not show any visible signs of receptivity, nor any expressions of gratitude or friendless in return. That is as it is and regardless, they will be uplifted by your caring smile, your thoughtful exchange, be it a word or a glance or simply through being in the vicinity of your presence even without direct interaction.

Dear Ones, much has been discussed as to the nature of mankind and the effects the dark influence has upon humanity. It is with a heavy heart that some are not responsive to the love you hold due to their imprisoned minds and hearts. This being said I, Archangel Metatron, shall assist those who suffer the slings and arrows of dire sorrow and pain, by pouring immense light into their soul streams to open them to the Truth of their Beings. And you, Dear Lightworkers, shall fortify and strengthen their ability to express love through your own example of loving presence. It is not for us to judge others in that we may feel some are more open than others. It is for us to simply emanate our love out into the world and So It Is.

Dear Ones, do know when I say that 'all is well,' this applies to the entirety of the earthly plane and all sentient beings. It may be challenging to discern as to whether or not your heart is shining love at times for you are focused upon activities that require your attention, and you are not focused upon you heart's ability to emanate love. This is all right for when you intend to maintain a loving stance throughout your day, then you will naturally maintain this balance of active compassion in all that you do, and so do not feel that you must be consciously focused upon sending love in order to do so.

To be a loving person is a way of being and a way of communication with everyone. Be it a plant, a person, an animal, you have only love to express as you are embodying your loving essence through your natural ability to exist in love. You see, Dear Ones, it is for you to live in peace and harmony in all that you do. So in living a life of love and peace, you experience great joy in being. It is for you to live a happy life with the confidence that all is well in the world, and that the contribution you make in uplifting and healing the hearts of humankind is simply a natural way of being. For you are like a flower unfolding its petals and opening to the beauty of natural sunlight and So It Is.

We are now at an impasse at this point in time, and so do make a conscious intention to maintain a loving stance throughout your day, and all will benefit from your presence regardless of whether or not you are interacting with someone or something or simply just being present. Do know that your loving stance is beneficial to you as well for this love flowing through your Soul from the Heart of Creator is healing and uplifting to you as you begin to embrace this energetic connectivity more and more and more.

Dear Ones, I say to you do be in Peace and do be in Love. For this is the key to heavenly expression in being, and it is natural and simple to reside within the divinity of your soul and thus, you become as gods walking upon the Earth anchoring vital nourishment and healing to all you encounter. All is well Dear Ones. All Is Well.

When you encounter someone who is not aligned with the truth of their divinity, it is well and good for you to share a word or glance of accepting love for who they are, and this in turn encourages them to accept themselves, bringing them closer to their inner truth. Dear Ones, and I reiterate the notion that all is well often so that your subconscious mind accepts this truth, and in doing so you become more confident that this is so. And you may be free of suffering the conflictual energetic exchanges in your life when you emanate only love, for this is reflected in your reality and your experience in the outer planes of being.

You see it is for the best for you to consciously intend to play this part in being the natural expression of Creators Divine Essence, for this is who you truly are, and this is the essence of who you are as well. Do exist in love in every moment, and you shall reap much joy and happiness in your life, for you shall experience greater love and light than ever before. Do open your hearts and minds wider, Dear Ones, to receive more and more and more magic and expansive consciousness in being.

It is without hesitation that I, Archangel Metatron, call upon you in service to the One, for it is written in the tablets of old that you shall rise at this juncture into the Heavenly Ascension of earthly transformation, and you are integral to this process, and do know it is so, Dear Ones. It is so on Earth as it is in Heaven through the presence of your Divine Love as you walk upon your sphere of global existence. And So It Is.

68

Take A Walk In Nature Today And Everyday

EVERY TIME you stop to observe a flower or a rock or anything of natural beauty, you may find there is a moment of wonder and a moment of reflection of what is innate to your natural existence in being. It is because you have an affinity for your natural environment, and you also have a natural attraction to your environment because in reality you are not separate from it. You see, Dear Ones, it is due to your knowing that everything around you is a reflection of your inner beauty and worth, as you are One with All That Is, and so to see yourself in all the beauty of nature is natural and appropriate for you are the divinity you experience within and without.

Every time you glance at a cloud in the sky or see a rainbow of multicolored rays, you are witnessing your own inner truth, and so it is no surprise that you would become more attuned to your own being in the presence of natural growth and expression of nature. Listen to your innermost thoughts and your innermost response to the natural environment provided through the Grace of Mother Earth, for she is the soul provider of all physicality in your earthly domain, and she appreciates your conscious connection to her. And when you find you are in complete and total resonance with your natural surroundings, you will experience peace and joy and simple pleasure of seeing the beauty around you.

Dear Friends, it is for your best and highest good to spend much time in the out of doors as this is energizing and enriching for your body and spirit. It is sometimes thought that the natural environment holds creatures and insects and other forms of undesirable experiences that could be of harm to you, and so there is resistance in being fully present with your natural environment.

Should you release your resistance and fear that you may be harmed in some way in moving through the wilds of nature, you will indeed experience the joy of being in an environment of beauty and radiant power manifest from the very heart of your own soul. As the world in its natural state exemplifies the unity and harmony of all things growing and coexisting together as one entity living interdependently, as all integral life forms are dependent upon the sustenance from Mother Earth. Thus, in this state of trust and peace no harm may come to you.

You see, Dear Ones, it is for me to remind you of your natural state of being, so that you may exist in peace and resonance with the world as you journey through it. To understand the unity of your own being with that of the entirety of the Earth will enhance your sense of peaceful presence. And also know that your entire environment is supportive of your existence, for without which you could not manifest physically in your dimensional expression of your truth.

You see there is much to draw from in this discourse, for those who isolate themselves from nature are separating themselves unknowingly from the wholeness of their being. To live without enjoying and interacting with the natural world is to cut off, in a sense, your life force from the earthly energetic flow. It is mandatory to connect to the Earth's magnetic field daily in order to maintain your energetic health so as to thrive and grow, just like the beautiful flowers around you do, as they are deeply rooted in the Earth.

I feel you understand what I say here, and I feel you know the truth of this. And so, Dear Ones, do intend to allow time daily to exist in a natural setting so that you may absorb and flow with the natural energetic expression of who you are in essence, so that you become connected to the energetic electrical flow manifest from the heart of your Mother Earth. For you are all beings of light and love and of biologic origin, and thus you have a great affinity for the world around you. I say this not only because it is true, I say this because it is essential that you connect with this natural flowing essence. For your physical body is dependent upon this energetic connectivity to the Earth, and so in order to maintain your physical health you may wish to make spending time in nature a part of your daily regime.

Do know that when you are in the presence of nature, you are in the presence of God manifest through the divine feminine expression of creation and birth. As the cycles of the Earth are infinitely expressing this truth of manifest living form and structure for you all to experience for the simple magnificent experience of living on the earth, and to not allow time to reap the benefits of living in nature is one of dire discontent. For you are not fully present in the world without the acknowledgement of your interdependent state of being in the world. And so it is essential for you to understand and know the unity you experience when you unite with the magnetic connection to your mother of all life upon the Earth.

Now it is time for you to realize the importance of being fully present with nature. So when you are in the forest or the planes or upon the shores of your continents, you can relax in the knowing you are safe in your natural environment, and so I, Archangel Metatron, shall assist should any illusive fears arise. For when you are in my loving embrace, you shall be protected, and you only need call upon me for this assurance and So It Is.

Every living being on Earth, who knows that they are unified in the glory of Creator's manifestation of natural beauty in all its forms, shall experience a deeper connectivity to your home planet, as it is essential that you are grounded as Lightworkers in healing the planet and all sentient beings existing around you. For the grounding is essential for energetically anchoring the energies necessary for this healing. As the energetic transmissions from the inner planes need you to be connect firmly into the Earth, so that those of us who assist your work may have a conduit of Light anchored into the depths of your planetary sphere.

Now do go out into the beauty of nature. Regardless of where you are there shall always be trees and plants and soil for you to connect into so that you are grounded, and also in a state of loving resonance with your home planet which you so desire to heal, and assist in ascending into the truth of all existence. Blessings as you walk upon the earthly domain of Loving Grace and So It Is.

69

Acceptance And Love Is The Key To Creating The New Paradigm

PERHAPS YOU MAY FEEL forlorn at times due to the global upsets and seemingly unjust treatment of beings upon your planet. The innocent appear to suffer; however, they do not do this out of victimhood. They choose to experience this traumatized experience for their personal growth as they are still encapsulated within the dualistic systems of behaviors belonging to lower dimensional existence.

It is heartbreaking indeed to see injustice prevail when it would be so easy to simply exist in peace. This is difficult to understand for Lightworkers who do exist in peace and loving presence. It does seem rather insane for anyone to harm another, and so it is difficult to comprehend why this is so. It is so, Dear Ones, because it is not for us to choose for others the reality they choose to experience.

Upon your planet is the opportunity to live freely, and so everything one desires to experience is allowed. Thus, one has the ability to correct their misalignment at any moment if only they choose to dissolve the illusions they hold as manifest in their reality. It is for each individual aspect to choose their journey in awakening, and everyone is on this journey that eventually leads to the Truth of their own Being.

So be it to say, that some shall continue their existence plagued by past karmic outplay of dire suffering chosen through their indoctrination of cultural fear, and wrongful acts misaligned with Creator's loving presence within, and so it is not for them to awaken at this juncture. For they have chosen more experience within the vibratory fields of dualism and conflict, and this is their choice, and it is perfectly suited for their evolutionary needs that will eventually unfold so as to lead them back to the truth of their own being.

You see, Dear Ones, it is inevitable that everyone shall ascend at some point in this outplay of karmic experience. You yourselves have traversed the highs and lows of dualistic existence, and only now do you see through the illusions prevailing in that perspective of reality. You have chosen peace, not conflict. You have chosen love, not hate. You have chosen truth, not falsehood. And so it is your time to transcend the illusions of dire suffering and pain that results from the free will choice of those who exist in fear and conflict.

Do know that although you may feel great sorrow for those who suffer, it is not for you to suffer the slings and arrows belonging to others who are still in the process of awakening. It is for you to experience compassion and understanding and acceptance for the state of the world's suffering. Indeed it appears now that things are getting worse and not better, however I assure you this is not the case. For things are improving and there is tremendous grace pouring into your earthly sphere, and so it is not to be obscured by the delusional perception that all is not well in the world.

Indeed, Dear Ones, all is well in the world, for it is for those who suffer still to continue their education, so to speak, so as to allow them to move into greater alignment with Creator's Grace, and what needs to transpire in order for this to happen does. And again it is through the free will choice of each individual, and not something that can be controlled or manipulated. What may be done is to send light to the hearts of those enmeshed in the turmoil so as to accelerate their awakening, for loving intent to focus light in areas of darkness does not interfere with free will choice. It simply gives light to the situations and beings so as to illuminate the truth and clarity within their being, to the extent they are open to it.

So sending love and light is not a violation nor an interference to the experience of another, as it can only serve to illuminate their perception of truth. Thus, your work is invaluable in service to humankind, and I encourage you, Dear Ones, to send love everyday to those in need, for I, Archangel Metatron, shall assist in all your loving intentions in all ways possible, as you are anchoring upon the Earth plane this desire to heal and mend the broken hearts of those who suffer and So It Is.

Peaceful and nonresistant behavior is the key to accepting the way the world appears, in knowing that all is unfolding perfectly. As the Creator has ordained that All Beings upon and within the Earth achieve liberation from the dual systems in place, so that eventually all will be free from fear and pain and will exist in the bliss of enlightened awareness. This is yet to be fully realized from your perspective along your current timeline. However, it is so in the dimensional perspective outside of your timeline. It Is So.

Please find solace for now, in the knowing that all is well upon the Earth, and do not be thrown from your heart centered stance by startling news of dire stress and unjust circumstance. It will continue for a time yet, and so do take care to align with your truth, and do not become embroiled in conflict nor upset when awareness of more turmoil arises.

Do not fear for all is well. Do not rise to anger nor dire stress for all is well. All is well, Dear Ones. All Is Well. Be at peace throughout your day and night in the knowing that all is well. Peaceful coexistence within a world of conflictual energies is possible, and not only possible, but essential in order to initiate the new paradigm of loving harmonious life on Earth. And So It Is.

70

Events Unfolding Upon The Earth Shall Not Waver The Love Of Divine Grace

EVENTIDE THERE IS A RAY OF HOPE upon the horizon so that all of humanity shall rejoice, for it is a ray of illumination and beauty within the hearts of all beings upon the Earth who awaken into a greater awareness of what is transpiring within the inner and outer planes of existence. It is known that in the unfoldment of the ascension process all will be healed and whole, existing in the loving embrace of the elemental design of Creator's Grace. And so it can be understood that all who read this discourse are to be free of all lower vibrational conflictual energetic hindrance and imbalance.

It is to be known that all who reside within their hearts in loving compassion and ceaseless presence of their inner truth shall ascend in various ways determined through soul desire of what is for their best and highest good. And all of those who wish to ascend have simply to read this discourse and practice the suggestions here to meet all future challenges that arise within their field of experience, so as to transcend and transform their stance into perfect balance and loving presence.

Peaceful coexistence within a world of turmoil can be a challenge indeed, and so I, Archangel Metatron, shall assist you in all ways to maintain your inner equilibrium so as to achieve balance and integral connectivity to the One of All That Is. Thus, you may maintain your ability to exist in loving acceptance of the free will choice of everyone who wishes to express their own passage of karmic interplay within their external reality.

It is known in Heaven that all shall be redeemed in time. However, for now, those of you who understand the ongoing process of Ascension shall experience more and more love and embodiment of Creator's I AM presence. This shall sustain you and protect you and guide you through the chaos and confusion abounding in various areas of the world, where dual systems play out karmic events that will become unbelievable to those who exist within their Christed Hearts, as they may not be able to comprehend the course of events unfolding before their eyes.

It is not for you to experience this chaos nor suffering, as you are in step with the ascending paradigm of loving peace upon the Earth. And so do take solace in the knowing that all is well, and there is no need to become enmeshed in the sudden shifts and changes in the landscape of humanities destined resolution of karmic outplay stemming from eons of time spent in dualistic behaviors.

It is meant for you to maintain a loving stance and one of acceptance, while at the same time take compassionate action to send the powerful light from your beings out into the world, for this shall uplift the frequency of the collective mind. Thus, all Beings on

Earth shall benefit and receive with ease this light without interference of free will choice. You see this is the key to not interfere with anyone's chosen experience. However, it is of immense help to those who suffer to have more loving light brought into the earthly realm so as to illuminate their direction, and uplift their clarity of mind.

Do realize that there is much to gain through your lightwork in that you are indeed a valuable part of the healing process unfolding upon the Earth. For there can be no joy in living a life of peace and love without sharing this stance with all you encounter. It is in the sharing of this love that joy is manifest, for generosity and caring is essential in embodying the infinite flow of Creator's Divine Grace.

You see, Dear Ones, your desire to give of yourself in order to assist others is the element of Creator's Grace, in that this flow of light to heal All hearts is indeed a blessing to all receiving it through their ability to open even the smallest amount. Although many do not appear to be receptive, it is still having an effect on some level of their being, and at some point this illumination shall manifest within their hearts and minds.

Be It Known on this day, that all who seek the Kingdom of Heaven on Earth shall arise and ascend through their loving hearts, regardless of what karmic circumstance they reside within. For all shall be redeemed who so choose the path into the light of higher dimensional existence. It is so Dear Ones. It Is So.

And so now you realize the impact your lightwork has upon the world and those who exist in, not only turmoil, but also illusion, for they have yet to awaken to the truth of their beings. It is for some, however not all, to ascend with the earth. For some have chosen to experience more incarnations within a dual environment, and this is well and good for they shall continue their evolutionary journey into the Heart of Creator's Divine Essence.

Please understand it is not unloving to allow others to choose what they deem to be for their highest good regardless of how things appear. It is for you to simply accept and send love to those who suffer, and to relinquish all doubt and fear and traumatized perception so that you may all exist in the loving acceptance and loving grace of Creator's Divine Presence here on Earth. And so it is on Earth as it is in Heaven.

Do know that time is of the essence, and that your focus upon uplifting the consciousness of humanity will allow many to ascend who would not have otherwise. Do appreciate the power you hold, and also the compassion for those who suffer. It is for you to share the gifts unfolding into the very core of your being. It is for you to discern when it is appropriate and good to send your healing love out into the world, and it is for you to discern what you are guided to express as world healers of Light and Love. And So It Is.

71

To Become Liberated Is To Open Your Hearts To Creator's Divine Grace

FAR AND FEW BETWEEN are the days numbered along the parameters of your reality encompassing much grief and turmoil, and so it is recommended you take solace with those of like mind to support you in the coming days and years ahead. For you may thrive and live in peace and loving presence, although much turmoil shall reign front and center within your media outlets and in various places throughout the world.

The upset is due to the culmination of all karmic outplay of dire repercussions due to conflict and suffering from eons past and present. You see, Dear Ones, it is inevitable that some shall perish in the flames of misfortune and recompense; however, all shall be redeemed in the time they have chosen, and so without fear and without grief you may exist in this knowing. Also, you may orchestrate more avenues to assist others who are seeking awakened stance by allowing yourselves to be moved through compassionate action in coming to their aid.

It is not for you to save the world. It is, however, for you to come to the aid of those who open their hearts in seeking solace in the peace you emanate. As to them the opportunity still exists to receive the attunement and the upliftment through Creator's grace and mercy, for they shall inherit the Earth as a home of beauty and love and joy without a trace of dire conflict nor suffering as far as their eyes may see. For it is to them to open their hearts and seek the wisdom of love within their own beings so that they may exist also in peace and loving presence.

You do now see, Dear Ones, the times of great disruption is upon you and all of the world, as the dark influences draw their presence here on Earth to a close, for they may not exist within this realm much longer as they have overstayed their karmic arrangements as it is. And this arrangement is one of prior claim to this earthly paradise for their own purposes for their self aggrandizement as separate entities, of which can only exist through illusive constructs, such as your governmental disempowerment of the masses leaving them without awareness of their own sovereignty in being.

This contract is no longer valid, as they have over extended the time they previously won to control the earthly sphere, and so they must pull up stakes, so to speak, and exist elsewhere in the Universe where Creator has deemed it appropriate for their evolutionary growth. For even those of dark origin exist within the loving embrace of the Creator, and it is ordained that they also have the free will choice to receive the Grace of Creator's Mercy.

For within their plans to control and enslave the earthly realm for their own advantage, there have been born numerous sparks of light that have opened avenues for liberation from their presence here. These sparks of light have created a powerful presence that cannot be obliterated by the dark manifest agenda, and so it is a credit to the human race that they have not collapsed into total darkness and dire fear in living.

The light has never been totally extinguished, for always there are those who carry the torch of truth forward, as you now see fully illuminating your entire planet. For the dark is not capable of overcoming the Light, and the Light can easily extinguish the dark. It is so here upon this planet within this particular timeline, that we see great miracles arriving daily to allow greater and greater amounts of light into the hearts of those who reside here.

It is for you to take joy in this victorious evolutionary development, as the dark recedes into the shadows no longer. There is too much light for the dark to hide, and so this exposure is bringing into the awareness of all who see with clarity what no longer works in this world of beauty and peace. And so this dark manifestation of karmic outplay shall boil over, so to speak, and disintegrate into the nothingness of transformative Love and universal power of Grace.

Now it is known upon the Earth as it is in Heaven, that all good hearted beings who open to this grace shall be redeemed in due time as they choose, for they have suffered long and can no longer be victimized by the viscous nature of dark origin. It is for those who seek a world of light to realize the potential of this present moment in the earthly history. As the dark recedes, the light envelops the hearts of all in awakening their minds and expanding their awareness of the Truth within their own Beings and Souls.

It is for us now to join in unity to confront all manifestations of darkness in loving acceptance, so that all resistance to pain and suffering dissolves in the Light of Truth. For no longer may the dark elements intrinsic to earthly experience exist here on this planet any longer, as they have overstayed their prior contractual claim on earthly control and domination of the hearts of those residing here currently, and also for those who have come before.

Now is the time for swift and knowing transformative action, so that all dark elements still existing here are completely irradiated. And so this is accomplished, Dear Ones, through your own loving hearts and through your own loving intentions for all to be healed and liberated that may emerge at this juncture. It is imperative that you all join in unity with the Beings of Divine Grace within and without the planes of existence, so as to liberate all who seek truth in existing upon the Earth.

It is for All to have this opportunity regardless of their karmic stance, for the Creator has ordained it to be so, and so it is. Through the free will choice of those who answer the clarion call to rise into the embrace of Creator's Love, to free themselves of all prior suffering and pain, so as to achieve liberation and evolve into the immense and miraculous presence of the One of All That Is. And it is so Dear Ones. It Is So.

Blessings to All reading this discourse, for I, Archangel Metatron, shall be at your side through the coming days and years to assist you through all trials and tribulations so that you shall achieve your heartfelt desire to ascend with your beautiful and magnificent Mother, the Earth. Know that regardless of what appears on your news outlets, there is much joy to experience in the liberation and upliftment of the Earth and those lovingly supporting her ascension process.

For she is One with all who rest upon her breast and she lovingly wishes for all to ascend with her. This being said, not all will, as they choose a different path at this juncture, a path leading inevitably to the same place, the Heart of the Creator. And so All Is well and good, in what appears to be a process of dire suffering for some. It is well and good, for all are in the ascension process sooner or later. The outcome is one of great joy and liberation for all who have suffered karmic repercussions on this planet and also any other planet. All Is Well and Good Dear Ones. Take solace in this knowing. And So It Is.

72

Knowing God Within Is To Know One's Self

FORMERLY KNOWN to humankind were loving voices of truth that were readily available to those who could hear within their own hearts and souls. And the voices were of divine manifestation whose purpose was to guide and to instruct various stages of spiritual development, and so there was a direct connection between all beings and their divinity within. Now it is so that most upon your planet are in a state of disconnect and are unable to hear this inner directive influence, and so it is a sad state of being when one believes themselves to be separate from the whole. For in truth there is no division in the Oneness of All That Is.

There is, however, a variety of manifest forms to experience different perspectives, and this experience was not meant to create the illusion of separation. Indeed it was intended to create the experience of the vast variety of forms available for soul growth and expansion. And so it is with great respect we give to all Sovereign Beings, as all forms manifest is an opportunity to realize greater awareness and creativity in being.

Be it known on this day, that all who seek the divinity within their own souls shall establish a connection to their divinity within, now and forever more, so that all illusion of separation falls away and they may be united within the Truth of their own Beings, and in time, shall become increasingly aware of this circumstance of existence. Although some may not open to this awareness, they shall still know they are not alone, and have loving support within the inner planes through their cognitive and intuitive ability to feel on a deeper level this truth within, albeit an unconscious one.

For in truth there is only one essence in being, and that essence is that of the creative force existing in all things manifest throughout this Universe and all Universes within the conscious mind of Creator. For all beings in existence, varied and miraculous in form, are indeed the embodied consciousness of the One of All That Is. This being we speak of is truly our own selves manifest in order to experience different perspectives and ongoing growth and development of our soul awareness in being.

Knowing who we are is the beginning of merging with the greater mind of the Creator, leaving behind all illusive obstructions that would prevent our embodiment of our true selves. And our true selves are the conscious mind of Creator who exists within all things and all forms of life within the inner and outer planes. You see, Dear Ones, there can be no us and them, for there is truly only the one presence within all beings. It is important to recognize that you are simply a part of an enormous whole of which cannot even be imagined, for the scope and breath of Creator's Being is beyond the comprehension of any single entity residing within or without.

The Creator is indeed a mystery to even those who embody great consciousness within the highest realms of being. Even I, Archangel Metatron, shall know no comprehensive experience of the Creator's totality in existence, and it shall remain a mystery until complete merging with the mind of Creator occurs when I am capable to perceive the immense nature of the Universe, and this capability will not occur while I remain within an individuated aspect of Creator's Expression. And so it is not known by any one single aspect manifest through individuated experience of one's own self, as the Creator is exploring, creating, and growing in breadth and width always and forever more, endeavoring to expand the conscious presence of the One of All That Is and So It Is.

It is through all the varied expressions of Creator's mindful presence that growth and expansion occurs, and it is through the free will choice of each individuated being that this growth occurs. For in the experience borne from different perspectives lives the eye of the Creator's all seeing, all knowing presence, experiencing through all manifest reality. It is difficult to imagine the scope of Creator's presence, and it is difficult to imagine the reality of Creator's existence as a single being. However, it is true and certain that the energy of love and the energy of light are one and the same, and uniting these frequencies is the vibratory sound reverberating throughout the entire essence of the Creator. We can only imagine, and yet this still does not validate the experience of actually being within the totality of the Creator.

We experience ourselves as separate aspects and so become entangled in the illusion of separation, however, this is not our truth. Our truth is that we are fulfilling soul requirements of experience to achieve balance and conscious presence of the Creator manifest throughout all beings within the One Mind of All That Is. We are not separate from God nor one another, and so the conflictual energies of dual behavior is indeed illusive, and creates the confused stance of your global circumstantial development that exists today in all parts of the world.

It is inevitable that someday the awakened ones become the centrifugal force upon the planet drawing all beings into higher consciousness, as they uplift the collective mind within the earthly planes into the totality of Oneness in Being. And this shift, as you refer to it, shall indeed spontaneously rise through the tipping of the scales so to speak, so that all beings are united in their coexistence upon and within your planetary sphere. It is to be a planet of beauty and uncorrupted, pristine expression of Creator's Essence evident throughout all who exist there. As All shall be One in this knowing with the deep respect for all life forms present as expressive of Creator's manifest reality in Being and So It is.

Suffice it to say, Dear Ones, the enormity of who you truly are is vast and expansive and powerful and loving, and so do have great respect and love for everyone and everything, as All embody the Creator's Divine Essence, and All shall rise into the conscious awareness of the inner divinity of Truth in Being here on Earth, just as it is in Heaven. And so it is Dear Ones, and So It Is.

73

Loving Discourse Uplifts Those Engaged In Conversation

UPON RISING in the morning it is well and good to breathe deeply and stretch your body so as to awaken your biologic processes. In this way you may reenter your dimensional physicality with increased presence so that you may carry throughout your day lightness in being. It is well and good to eat and drink substances that enliven your body and soul through the energetic exchange of nutrients and also through the exchange of oxygen molecular enlivenment.

It is well and good to look in the mirror and brush your hair and dress in a comfortable and clean manner, so as to put your best foot forward, so to speak, in meeting the day ahead. It is well and good to brush your teeth and care for your skin so that it remain moist and supple. The skin is of importance as it protects and heals itself when there is irritation or injury. It protects your internal organs and bodily functions as well.

It is well and good to always listen to your heart centered guidance, as to what steps to take where, as you journey forward. For internal guidance is essential in aligning with Creator's Divine Purpose in Being. It is recommended you bathe frequently to cleanse not only your skin, but also your energetic fields, as water has an etheric component that also bathes you energetically of all accumulated angst, fear, and dire worries existing in your fields. Exercise is also of utmost importance to maintain the strength and flexibility of the physical body and also to enliven your energetic bodies. It is essential for good health for daily maintenance to take place for everyone who wishes to experience ultimate health in being.

Not only diet and exercise are essential for good health, but also healthy mental practice so that one's thoughts uplift projected outlooks into the daily experience. For to worry or to fear or to engage in thoughtless conversation of lower vibratory discourse is indeed draining to one's energy, and also affects the frequency which you emanate out into the world. It is well and good for you, Dear Ones, to engage in conversation that is uplifting and nonjudgmental, so that your realm of influence may be affected in a loving and supportive stance. That is to say to always remember to hold the highest good for everyone in your hearts and minds and through the words you speak. In this way no harm is ever done to anyone or anything.

It is easy to fall into conversation with another who wishes to complain or express their confusion regarding a conflict in their life. It is not necessarily appropriate for you to respond in a manner which would indulge this behavior. In other words, entering into conversation that is not uplifting or loving would do harm energetically to whatever is being discussed directly or indirectly, as idle talk is of no value in healing and supporting the person speaking, nor someone being discussed. It is actually not beneficial to anyone to indulge their encumbering dialogue with you. It will ultimately drain and lower your vibration to attune to harmful discourse.

It is also wise to speak in terms of what is joyous and positive so as to direct the conversation to a more illuminating outlook on life. When someone wishes to unload, so to speak, upon you their grief or confusion you may simply say, lets view this from a higher perspective through examining the underlying cause of this distress or concern or whatever may be the topic. By introducing an alternative viewpoint borne of loving understanding can soothe and also heal the conversation of judgmental negativity.

Do understand that there may be opportunities to affect another's outlook, although it may have only a temporary effect. Still it is more purposeful to endeavor to uplift the focus of the verbal exchange through higher perspectives of what is right and loving and accepting, when another is at odds with someone or something. When all is said and done, then the receiver of this discourse may feel lighter in some way and also dissolve their conflictual stance upon the topic. Thus, more good is accomplished in this manner than simply listening to another's grievances and complying with their attitude through conversational exchange.

When you are out and about, always remain mindful of the impact you wish to create in greeting others, and become responsible for the effect you create in speaking to others. Yes, there are times when you are distracted or hurried; however, this behavior allows your unconscious response to those around you, which is not focused upon the best behavior considering all things happening at once.

For example, you may be late to an appointment and encounter a friend along the way. You do not feel you have time to engage in conversation, and so this encounter is inconvenient for you at that time. You may ordinarily respond by saying, "Good to see you, but I can't talk now as I'm late to an appointment." This is honest and also an efficient way to keep moving onward to your destined appointment. Another way of responding to this 'chance' encounter is to consciously greet them in love and appreciation of their presence and also to be consciously present with them, without having your attention placed upon a future event, which in this case would be to arrive at the appointment.

Instead, through being present with them connecting through loving presence, is for the best and highest good of both of you, for you may be aligned in the moment and can share uplifting love and unity in purpose, without having to engage in a long conversation. And then it would be fine to explain you are in a hurry to arrive somewhere and would love to talk later. You see, Dear Ones, the only difference in these two ways of encountering another in this situation, is that in one you are not present and existing in your loving presence, and in the other you are present existing in your loving presence.

No time is saved by not being present with another, you see. It takes the same amount of time to respond either way. However, when you respond in love and focus within the present moment, you are emanating light to another, and so this is for the highest and best good for all concerned. Whether you feel like speaking or not, being present in your loving stance is always the most beneficial to you yourself and to others, for you are experiencing your connectivity to everyone and everything and can reap the rewards of unity within all experience you encounter throughout your day. And so it is Dear Ones and So It Is.

74

Living In Peace Creates The Holy Land

BEFORE THIS TIME there were many means and ways to ascend spiritually that involved a life of devotion and spiritual practice. However, now there is a difference, in that all those who wish to grow and evolve need not commit themselves to a life of isolation nor solitude from the eyes of everyday reality within the earthly dimension. For now it is possible to transcend the earthly plane of dualistic systems through simply opening the heart and mind to direct transmissions of healing grace showering upon all who wish to receive.

It is not necessary that a particular name be called upon for divine deliverance or for one to engage in a particular religious perspective. It is only necessary to offer one's self in service, surrendering to divine love and compassion, for anyone to become transformed through the grace of the Creator. It is not difficult, as in times past to shake off the fears and pain of dual behaviors, for the grace will shed light in all areas of darkness illuminating truth and clarity in being. And so it is for those who seek the Kingdom of Heaven upon the Earth, for now we have reached an impasse that shall allow all who suffer to ascend should they simply choose to do so.

It is with great joy I, Archangel Metatron, bestow upon the millions who suffer avenues of grace so as to awaken the hearts of many who otherwise would not have experience of the opportunity to ascend from lower vibrational existence into higher realms of consciousness. It is needless to say that some will choose to ascend at a later time and space, as they require more lessons and experience to desire alignment with Creator's Divine Essence. It will be for them to journey on into realms appropriate for their evolutionary growth. Suffice it to say, all is well for them, as they will eventually experience Ascension through divine grace as well, for no one is ever excluded from the process of evolutionary growth.

And for anyone wishing to ascend with beloved Mother Earth, they have their path paved in gold so as to accelerate their development of conscious awareness within the vast expanse of Creator's loving presence. It is so for all who choose this regardless of their karmic stance to enter into the Kingdom of Heaven while embodied upon the Earth. As many shall fall, so shall many rise into the glory that is Thine Own Truth and there will be no illusion of separation evermore. For those who seek to open their hearts in loving acceptance of the earthly dimension as it is at this time, they will receive assurance and consolation that all is truly well for all, despite odd appearances of external stance.

You see, Dear Ones, it is not for you to suffer the slings and arrows of lower vibrational existence. It is for you to enjoy a magical and miraculous transformation of the earthly plane. For all dire suffering and pain shall exist no more, and only loving presence is experienced in all upon the Earth. Every Being shall experience their sovereignty in being and shall recognize the divine essence in everyone and everything. Even the animals, now considered to be lowly beasts, shall be known for their enlightened presence expressed in multitudinous forms, and they shall be free of all suffering and pain inflicted upon them by humanity and other forms of aggressive animal behaviors.

For only love shall be present, and only respect and generosity shall be the premise for all communicable exchange. It shall be Heaven on Earth, Dear Ones. So do not give into despair or hopelessness as the appearance of transformation takes place, for all is well, Dear Ones. I repeat, All Is Well. Do take a deep breath and recite, "All Is Well." For the truth shall set you free, and it is all right if this knowing is not currently clear in your minds. Open your hearts to loving in every moment and you shall become this Truth. Yea, the Truth shall set you free.

It may not be apparent how all of the seemingly dire circumstances are an unfoldment of divine grace. However, it is for you to trust without fearful reservation, that those who wish to ascend shall, regardless of what is communicated to you on your news outlets. For they only provide a small inkling of what is really transpiring globally, and certainly none of the powerful and beautiful transmissions of uplifting grace taking place continually upon your planet. So do not be dismayed should you tune into your governmental controlled media outlets, for this will not really present the truth of your global stance, and there will be no televised coverage of the Earth's Ascension that reach the masses. Indeed only you shall know through attuning yourselves to the inner truth 'network' so to speak, and there you shall receive guidance as to the reality of what is transpiring globally.

It is not for you to suffer any longer the strife and sorrows of dimensional suffering of times past. It is for you, Dear Ones, to exist in peace and loving existence, so as to reside now in the new paradigm of worldly peace and harmonious coexistence. It is for you to send your love and light into all areas of dire pain and suffering, so as to lessen the grip of dark control upon those who suffer still. This compassion may take place even while you exist in a state of love and joy, for it is not to ignore or become indifferent to the suffering still playing out. It is through your loving compassion that light permeates the dark and so the Earth shall rise into higher dimensional expressions of peace and transcendent healing love for All.

Eventide shall resolve all sorrow and blame, and peace shall reign once more upon the shores and banks of all the world, for Love is the answer. Only your love and the love manifest from the Highest of the Holies within, shall reign supreme upon your lands to exist in total peace everywhere, within everyone, and everything, human and animal alike. For all is manifest of Creator's Mind and Heart, and All shall sing the song of the ages now and forever more. Do realize there is no greater healing than that of loving light for it permeates the dark and heals all the wounds that would hinder growth and evolvement. It is so Dear Ones. It Is So.

75

Peace Exists Within The Loving Hearts Of Those Who Emanate Grace

DEAREST ONES OF ALL the earthly domain, I seek your attention, for now you have arrived at an impasse and there is no going back. No going back to the old perceptions of times past. No going back to the irretrievable lack of knowing that All Is One and One Is All. For in this knowing there is the substantial acquisition of knowledge that will sustain you in the days ahead amid much chaos and confusion.

Do know I, Archangel Metatron, am with you always to sustain your sense of peaceful knowing and loving stance whilst others may still appear lost or even forgotten. I assure you they are not, for the Creator is always present within every manifest being and soul here on Earth and throughout the Universe. It is for you to understand that there shall always be paths of redemption and solace within the hearts of all should they choose to follow them, whence they are ready.

For long has it been upon your planet that the people and animals have suffered greatly and I, Archangel Metatron, shall always be present within the hearts and minds of all to lead them back to their source of origin, and this source, of course, is the Creator of All That Is. For there can be no separation within the One

Mind and One Heart of God that prevails throughout all existence, throughout all experience, throughout all timelines, throughout all lifetimes, and throughout the inner planes of all dimensional existence. For All is encompassed within Creator's breadth and width and dimensional expansion throughout all time and space.

As the Creator is indeed You and is indeed All whom you encounter in this world and within your inner sanctum. For there is nothing less nor more, than the precious and beautiful and loving presence of God manifest as loving light permeating all space and all time. For in time, there is the perception of true movement of the unfoldment of Creator's Grace to experience all the unraveling of creative manifest expression into all forms of existence, and within all forms manifest is the Heart and Soul of the One of All That Is. There can be no separation, nor less significance to any form manifest, for the Creator resides within All as the same essence and presence.

And so it is for you to realize that all life and all forms of life are precious and worthy of caring respect, and acknowledgement of the truth within all things. It is for you to acknowledge and to ascertain your ability to give loving light to all things and all beings you meet in your journey of time as it unfolds before your eyes. It is imperative to give of one's heart and soul as this light awakens the hearts around you. For Life is indeed precious regardless of its form, and it deserves the utmost respect regardless of the consciousness present within it, for many are sleeping, and many are still in this unfoldment of the passage of time that leads to greater awareness eventually and inevitably into the Heart of the One.

Do realize that although not everyone appears receptive, it is essential that you, Dear Lightworkers, uphold your loving stance to all regardless of whether they may appear to be heart centered within their lives or not. For no one is to be excluded from love, just as no one is excluded from the embrace of Creators Loving Essence, and this exemplifies your own self acting as the Divine Essence of the Creator within your very own Being. For you may grow and expand the conscious presence of the One within only through your loving recognition of the divine grace within, as to who and what you truly are.

There can be no separation nor judgment of anyone or anything, as this creates the illusion of separation, and there is in truth, none. For all the world is One in divine manifestation, and the suffering you see in the world is due to this lack of awareness of the true nature of all things manifest. Amid this confusion and disconnectivity many fall into despair; however, Dear Ones, your loving stance and continual emanation of your inner truth shall set them free. Yes, you are this powerful, and you have received this same love you emanate out into the world. For your awareness is born of this loving grace received, just as you continue this flow of loving grace out into the world in all its forms, and this includes all plant life and animal life and marine life and all elemental expressions of Creator's manifest reality upon and within the Earth.

As Mother Earth ascends, so shall all Beings wishing to ascend with her into the New Paradigm of earthly existence of harmonious rapture and bliss, in being of conscious recognition of the unified presence of Creator's Love within All. Yes, this is Heaven on Earth, and this is indeed the reality that Ascension leads One and All into, so that all acknowledges the unity of all things. It is beautiful and true and right that one resides within this amazing and miraculous world of loving existence, a world born of dire trust that all is well. And So It Is Dear Ones that All Is Well.

For now in the Heavens and upon the Earth, the timeline is viewed where this is so for all who ascend into the marvels of higher dimensional existence. This is so for you, as you journey onward through your loving hearts and minds of unified presence. This is so, for those who suffer still the experience of dual behaviors, at a juncture that is appropriate for them when they so choose. This is the way of the Universe. It has always been and shall always be the unfoldment of divine grace allowing free will choice, and this is the beauty of individual sovereignty within the embrace of Creator's Loving Essence, so all may experience divine aligned existence through their own volition of choice. This is Divine Freedom and This is Divine Love. And So It Is.

76

Recent Events Foretell More Confusion Transpiring Upon The Earth

RECENT EVENTS FORETELL more confusion and sordid acts of vile retribution from the dark influence upon the powers of governmental control. And so, Dear Ones, do not be alarmed or discouraged for there is wondrous energetic influx of divine grace flowing upon all on planet Earth, so that these monstrous acts are vindicated through healing love and karmic clearance of traumatized experience.

Be that as it may, for now there is great suffering among the masses who are imprisoned by the forces of control that oppress those on Earth, and it is only through one's loving heart may they be rescued. It is not enough to hold space for peaceful resolution. This global situation requires action, and also strength to rise up in the face of adversity and tumultuous circumstance. You see, by sending healing love to all areas of dire suffering, there can be tremendous assistance from the inner planes of Divine Grace. It is through your own volition that you may engage the higher powers of divine grace and love to heal and permeate the darkness violating the rights of all beings.

What is required is its askance. And so, Dear Ones, do ask me, Archangel Metatron, and any and all Divine

Beings of great power and knowing, for assistance in resolving the dire conflictual energetic dissonance presence in your plane of existence. Please know that in doing so you will engage the assistance of multitudinous Angelic Realms in Being, so that great force and power are enacted to intercede the dark influences that wish to undermine the ascension process for your beautiful planet and all upon it.

Reason is not permitted within the dark minds of those who are possessed by dark influence. Reason is not permitted within the perpetrators of crimes of great suffering inflicted due to this dark inhabitation of controlling regimes long established in your world. For they are void and completely bereft of all emotional sensitivity to those of whom they inflict suffering upon, and so do not delay to call on us, the Divine Intermediaries, to bring clarity and love and healing to your planet surface, for you have the power to ask of your free will choice and then it can be so.

Through taking action in asking for our assistance during this dire uprising of dark elemental control, we can united, bring great power to those in the positions of leadership who may have the opportunity to override the dark controls of the current regime. And this being said, I, Archangel Metatron, shall abide by the heartfelt desire of those who call out for justice and liberation from their oppressors, as they reside upon the Earth at this time and at this juncture, so that All Beings may be free at long last of all discord and dissonance within the earthly sphere of existence.

This being said, do ask, Dear Ones. Ask everyday and every time you see or hear of great discord or disharmonious actions that are bereft of the health and beauty and loving stance of peace upon Earth. For even as those who seek restitution from governmental divisive action, shall indeed be assisted in uniting with their loved ones and So It Is.

Now it is known to all Lightworkers that they have great power in simply asking for assistance from the Divine Power of Loving Grace. And it is to be taken with great honor, to become available to transmit your divine intention to send love and healing throughout the world and throughout the Cosmos. For the energetic reverberations of this suffering inflicted upon your masses is far reaching creating great discord throughout the vibratory field of your entire Universe.

And so it is known that those who perpetrate these misdeeds shall be held responsible for their unconscionable acts of dire crimes enacted upon their people who have entrusted them with their power and leadership, so that these beings are no longer able to manifest their hold on those who suffer, and upon those who thrive in the new paradigm of conscious co-creation of peace and sovereignty in being on Earth. Be not afraid, Dear Ones, for their time is short and their influence is waning, so that the strength of love and healing shall override all terror and fear and dire suffering. All shall be redeemed through the Grace of Divine Creator and It Is So.

Dear Ones, suffice it to say, you are the ones who have the power to create the needed change on Earth and this power is within your hearts, and so do not hesitate to utilize and act every day. For everyday you shall rejoice in the knowing that all is well. As these dire manifestations of dark influence arise, so shall they pass away, and all shall be healed and recovered in the

Grace of Creator's Divine Upliftment. All shall pass and so All Is Well as you have been reminded of numerous times during these discourses.

The reason is truly simple, in that before this time there have always been tumultuous suffering and expressions of hate and fear, and so at this time you see the uprising of all the dark influence long present upon your planet so that all comes into the light of day. And in this Light all darkness dissolves and new life and new opportunity for divine manifestation of the truth within all beings shall reign supreme. It is so Dear Ones. It Is So.

Never be dissuaded from the truth and the knowing that all is well, for this shall sustain you and comfort you when you are bombarded by the media outlets reporting dire events of conflictual nature. You shall know that all is well, for I, Archangel Metatron, foresee your world evolving and overcoming the darkness of the ages and all shall exist in the perfect glory of Creator's intended existence upon the Earth. It Is So and So It Is.

Even though you have an idea of what may transpire in the future, do be assured that you are safe and secure throughout the coming days, and do remain in a stance of peaceful knowing that All Is Well, so that you may continue to manifest the new paradigm of peaceful coexistence in the world, and so it is, Dear Ones. And So It Is.

77

Needed Understanding
For Mother Earth's
Journey At This Time

DEAR ONES, TODAY I WISH to discuss matters of concern that create great sorrow within your minds and hearts. You do care deeply and truly for those innocent lives affected by the trials and tribulations generated through dark influence and dire dissonance within the nature of current events. It is not for you to suffer, although it is for you to know, that those who are seemingly innocent in being affected by dire circumstance of disruptive forces of dark interference are only innocent in that they have not created the situation at hand. You may as well know, that those who appear as innocent have karmic energetic outplay as well in most of these circumstances. And so they experience results of karmic debt so to speak, in that they have chosen to absorb the karmic intermingling of dire consequences borne of prior experiences, collectively and personally, due to the karmic nature of the human collective experience on Earth.

Be advised to allow yourselves to respond to these sorrowful outcomes with the natural caring and concern that is innate to your being. However, do not feel that there has been a mistake or an injustice, as many of these dire events of suffering are no more that the opportunity for those who are affected, to resolve old karmic patterns and old prior karmic debt for misdeeds enacted by them at some point in time. They are choosing to receive restitution and redemption for their involvement in the current karmic outplay that will release all of humanity and all of the Earth from previous misdeeds, due to unconscionable acts enacted without the awareness of their inner truth and their inner knowing of divine presence.

It is for you to realize that you are not affected personally due to your clear karmic slate, and you shall experience the new earthly paradigm of divine presence within all beings, great and small. For to experience your truth and your knowing within, is a result of your conscious choices to ascend with the Earth and with one another who reside within the Truth of their Beings.

It is for you to relish the beauty and majesty of the Earth and not be encapsulated by the grief and suffering during this transitional period of transformation. For all shall be redeemed through their own personal choices of what avenue they will journey upon to attain and align with the truth within their beings. And should you have followed this entire discourse up to this page of entry, you do understand all that is transpiring, and all that is to transpire, while holding on tight to the knowing of your loving heart and mind to sustain you during the times of chaos and confusion. For you realize and truly understand through your inner knowing that All Is Well.

Dear Ones, all is truly well. Do continue your beautiful Lightwork and your beautiful intentions to heal and repair and assist those who are open to receive your light, and this of course can be anyone or anything elemental in nature, be it in a living form or be it in the form of mineralized manifestation. As this will come into play in the future more and more as the body of the Earth requires your healing love and patience in her recovery process from eons of abuse by the human interference of her global state of being, as one of a natural and harmonious nature.

The Earth has suffered greatly of her own free will to withstand the trials and tribulations brought forth by humankind that have interfered with her existence, in that she has absorbed and contained great amounts of dark energetic grief and horror through the numerous wars, and the numerous excavations of her body, mind, and spirit, that have corrupted her natural physical and energetic flow. And now she can bear no more in her endeavor to give humanity the time it needs to find restoration of it true state of origin, and so she wishes to ascend for she no longer can carry this karmic weight without the desecration of her own Being.

So it is indeed time for the Grace of Creator to assist her in her quest to leave the lower dimensions in being so that she may heal and repair and restore her body and soul to its true nature in Being. She loves all residing upon her breast and wishes all who may, to ascend with her, as she lovingly assists all Lightworkers and all who choose Ascension who are complete in their lower vibratory journeys, for she is a Blessed Being of Great Light and accomplished stance. She is One with All That Is, and she chooses to continue her evolutionary journey into the Heart of the Creator.

And her choice to manifest as the great being she is, has been a culmination of much experience and much sacrifice to waylay her ascension journey, in order to allow time for those who are ascending with her to complete their third dimensional journey within her loving embrace. She has served great purpose in her tolerance and her forbearance in maintaining a nourishing and beautiful land for All. And now she must ascend in order to survive the continual interference within and upon her physical body, and she can no longer maintain the dire pain of holding the suffering of humankind through the ages, for it is of great destruction to her spirit and to her soul.

No longer may she reside in the conflictual realities of the lower dimensions, and so she chooses to ascend in order to journey with her beloved life forms who are indeed clear and devoted to her success in reaching the higher dimensional states in existence. The Earth is now free and in her ascension process, and so those accompanying her may rejoice for all is well. And do express deep gratitude to this magnificent Being of Loving Light and pristine nature for she will do well, along with your blessings upon her Heart and Soul. And So It Is.

Know that the time is near for Mother Earth to shift into higher dimensional consciousness and you, Dear Lightworkers and Beings who choose to exist in Love, are welcome to join in her shifts of dimensional upliftment. It is mandatory that all who ascend shall exist in a fearless state, for there is indeed nothing to fear, and this absence of fear shall open the gates of Heavenly Ascension for only Light exists in the higher dimensions of Being.

It is an easy and natural occurrence to ascend, you see, for it is no different than that of experiencing a flower blooming into the light of day. It is natural and will require no effort nor concern about worthiness, as all who exist within their loving heart will ascend with ease. It will unfold naturally and easily one day at a time as you continue to cycle with Mother Earth in her orbital path of spiraling into the higher dimensions.

It will feel as though you are becoming lighter and healthier and more joyous and more expansive, in a gentle and soft way that will not startle or upset your perception of reality. In fact, you will feel as though you are returning to your natural state of being and all will be well. Yes, all is well for all concerned, as all choose their own time to ascend, and for you, Dear Ones, the time is now. The time is now, and forever more do live in the knowing of joyous presence of the One of All That Is. And So It Is.

78

Eventide of Dark Influence Wanes And Soon Will Be No More

SUFFICE IT TO SAY, Dear Ones, that there are many and varied life forms existing upon the Earth today, and there have been as well in the ancient past and all in between that are in need of your loving light and healing, not only those who exist now, but also those who have lived in your historical past as you view from your current timeline. For now is the eternal moment always present, always now. There is no other reality than this.

This being said, I, Archangel Metatron, shall illuminate the truth of your timeline in that you exit within it, just as those you view in your past also currently live within their timelines. Indeed you may exist in more that your current timeline, for you see your entire existence contains all your lifetimes on this planet and any other planet at once.

This may be difficult to comprehend in that you perceive time as something passing from the present into the past, as though the past exists in your present as a memory. However, it is only the present moment that exists, and does not cease to exist simply because your present state of conscious perception no longer perceives it. For your consciousness does indeed move forward in the present moment to experience new unfoldment of ever changing circumstance, so as to expand your growth and your knowing of what is.

It is not always so for those on Earth to grow and expand, for they are enveloped in patterns that continue and do not allow for growth and new experience. You may say they are going nowhere, for they have limited perception of their self created reality. It is likened to the life of a muskrat who daily travails the same terrain in order to find food, and once finding it, they return to their home in the ground to await another day's hunger.

Some humans behave in a similar way in that they follow a pattern of behavior, and never allow this pattern to change, for they find comfort and security in existing in this predictable environment. It is not so for those who seek the truth of their existence, for they are open to new and unique experience that moves them forward in their understanding of life and the purpose of their existence on the Earth, and also are curious as to their relationship with the entire Universe.

Some will continue their patterned behavioral existence and some will not. And it is all well and good for eventually those encapsulated in a particular circumstance shall break through due to karmic opportunities to view life in new ways, and thus, they are free to move forward on their journey of truth in being. And so again I tell you all is well.

This all being considered in terms of existing at once everywhere traversed in numerous lifetimes, we see as a dilemma, for it is not possible to consciously exist everywhere at one time, or so it seems. In reality it is possible, Dear Ones, although not to your conscious mind, for your conscious mind is single focused upon your current now moment. So it is the movement of your conscious experience that creates the illusion of time.

Now this is not to say that your experience of the moment is illusion, for it is not. It is true and actual experience. However, the past experience still reverberates in its existence, and so it is also existing in the present moment although your conscious focus is no longer upon it. This is perplexing indeed for you who are not aware of the nature of existing everywhere at once. How can this be?

It can be, Dear Ones, for the dimensionality of all timelines and all lifetimes in all the varied and multitudinous forms existing now and for always, are simply vibrational experience in the form of energy that is vibrating eternally out into the Cosmos of All That Is. And so all the wonderful and beautiful experience along with experiences of grief and sorrow exist and reverberate out into the Creator's Universe for All Time created in the ever present now moment.

So you see that there is much to heal in what you regard as past experience, not only for yourself, but for the entirety of all existence within the entire Cosmos. And You, Dear Lightworkers, may also heal this energetic vibratory field that encompasses past sorrow and grief from the great suffering that has occurred throughout eons of time, as you perceive experience through the movement of your conscious focus in the now moment.

You may endeavor to seek assistance from myself, and from other and any Divine Beings of Loving Light, in order to heal the past suffering upon your planet throughout multitudinous lifetimes and timelines that reverberate out into the entire field of Creator's Being. This can be so through your simple intent to heal this condition of dire pain and suffering wherever it emanates out into the Cosmos, due to karmic misdeeds upon your planet throughout all time and space, throughout the entire existence of the Earth.

For there has not always been suffering upon your planet. In the ancient times of origin of life here on Earth, there were times of great joy and peace and harmony, as life was intended to be for all. Due to dark interference from other planetary systems where dark beings ruled and controlled their environment, they sought to extend their control over other planetary systems in order to obtain new avenues of resources that empower their existence of dark and dire intent.

These beings obtained a foothold here upon your planet and they are now at long last losing their grip upon the earthly domain, and so soon all traces of their dark imprintation shall disappear, dissolve, resolve, and also completely clear without a trace of ever having been here. This is because the Creator has deemed the planet Earth to be free of dark inhabitation and all infestation within the hearts and minds of those who suffer their presence still.

It is time in this present moment, for all Lightworkers to unite in their intention to heal all sorrow and grief and fear that has ever been created upon this planet, and I, Archangel Metatron, shall implement the healing of all past karmic misdeeds and the suffering created through these acts everywhere as they reverberate throughout the entire Cosmos and Beyond and So It Is.

79

Now Is The Time To Know
You Are Free Forever More

EVERY ONCE IN A BLUE MOON, there is an opportunity to revise, review, and relinquish all prior conflictual energies so that your slate is clear, and that opportunity is now, Dear Ones. Now is the opportunity to obtain clarity in being so that all past turmoil and conflict in your lives is dissolved and relinquished, so that you may move forward in peace and inner knowing that all is well.

You see it is inevitable that some may not ascend, and this is well and good, for it is not in the divine flow of their development and evolutionary journey at this juncture. However, you who read these words are called into alignment with your ascension pathway so that now, and for always, you reside within your inner truth and inner heart of compassion and love.

I, Archangel Metatron, shall assist you in all ways to clear your path of any and all roadblocks, so to speak, so that you may ascend and traverse your unique soul pathway without fear of dire pain and suffering. For your time of suffering is at an end, and now you may reside in the beauty and knowing that you are free, Dear Ones. Peaceful coexistence is upon the horizon, and at long last you are free to ascend into the heavens of the higher realms of conscious existence, and this is not to fear but to rejoice in. For you are returning to your original state of Being and So It Is.

It is not for you to suffer any longer, regardless of the experience some will continue to have so as to further their developing evolvement of the third dimensional dual existence. It is often that you may wonder how this process works, and I assure you that you have a natural sense of the growth taking place within your being and soul. For you are likened to a rose whose petals softly open to the light, and so you are the rose, and you are the light, and So It Is.

Do not hesitate to call upon me should you relapse into a state of fear or confusion, and I shall uplift your spirit, body, and soul into the clarity you seek. For thine is the grace manifest upon Earth as it is in Heaven. And this is a lovely way to think of this process, for it is a process of eternal growth and eternal salvation from all dark influence evermore.

You see, Dear Ones, it is essential you relinquish all fear and doubt as to where your path leads, for you are headed into the Heart of Creator's Loving Essence, and this is where there is no longer suffering nor pain nor grief nor conflict. For you now fully connect into the field of the One of All That Is. The field of love, the field of light, being one and the same essence, for the Creator is the All of existence everywhere, and you now may experience the vastness of this expression throughout the entire Universe and Beyond.

The Creator is none other than your own selves existing in loving presence and peaceful coexistence. It is now you realize You are the Heart and Soul of the Creator, now and always within your diverse expressions of divine manifestation. You may fully and completely relax, Dear

Ones. Take a deep breath, and know that all is well and good in the world, although external circumstance would otherwise appear, for you now understand all you need to understand in order to ascend in the acceptance that All Is Well for One and All.

It is the eventide of events unfolding upon the Earth, and upon the breast of Mother Earth all is well. For the ascension process is well underway, and the process is unfolding at increasingly rapid rates throughout the entire planet and, yes, also the entirety of your Universe. For this Ascension happens, not only to your planet and those upon it. It also happens everywhere at once so that all may expand and grow and experience more of the wonder and awe of Creator's Divine Presence.

You may visit vast and beautiful vistas of lands unknown, here on this planet, and also everywhere within the inner planes. You shall develop the ability to travel through your energetic form to other star systems to partake in their environment, and experience Creator's magical means to manifest in new and varied forms of expression. It is so, Dear Ones. As impossible and as unimaginable as it sounds, It Is So. For you are no longer bound by the dictates of a closed system of reality. Only freedom of existence is your domain, and within this domain all is possible, and your ability to traverse the Universe holds no limits upon your ability to do so.

You are set free, Dear Ones, and what this means is that you experience great joy in Being and have total freedom of movement anywhere and everywhere. Take a deep breath and contemplate what this means now. This means you are free of all lower vibrational energetic experience of dire stress and pain and fear. You are free, and I cannot emphasize this enough, for you no longer live within the confines that has bound you for centuries from the Truth of Who You Are.

Within and without, You are an expression of the Glory of the Creator, and there are infinite possibilities as to how you choose to advance your knowledge and expand your energetic ability to hold greater and greater amounts of light. This is the moment you have been wishing for. This is the moment you have longed for and yet did not realize would come in this way. For living on a planet in physical form and ascending with your beloved planet is new and invigorating and enlivening.

For all who acquire this book shall know it is your time to Ascend. And to ascend without fear of the unknown is simply to open to greater love and greater light, and all will transpire and transform with ease and childlike joy. For thine is the child of Creator's Love and Creator's Expression, and you shall have multitudinous experiences of growth and expanded awareness from here on, Dear Ones. Rejoice for You are the Ones who live in Freedom Everlasting. You are the Ones who shall ascend with the Earth, and shall reap the benefits of your long journey endeavoring to uplift the beings upon your planet, and it has been a long road indeed. And now this journey is at an end, for you stand upon the precipice of great advancement and great joy in Being.

This is no surprise that you are ready to let go of everything that has hindered your freedom in becoming sovereign and existing in the truth that you truly are and have always been. You are now at the pinnacle of achievement in rising out of the confusion and conflict of dire suffering in the dual system of existence. Every time you think of past traumatized experience, know that it is no more. You no longer are bound karmically nor collectively, to the suffering you once endured. Dear Ones, you are free. I repeat, You Are Free. Know this. Be this. Accept the Joy awaiting you as you continue your never ending journey in Peace and Freedom and Love. It is so Dear Ones. It Is So.

80

For Now The New Paradigm Exists On Earth As You Ascend Into The Heavenly Realms

TODAY OF ALL DAYS is the day of reckoning for Lightworkers everywhere, for they shall inherit the Earth: the Earth of peaceful, loving cohabitation within All Beings present within and upon her. For she is ascending, and as she ascends, she accelerates her process, and all in discord and all existing within the confines of dual behavior shall be no longer upon this Earth. For they shall take up residence in other star systems where they may arrive into similar circumstance they now experience; however, they shall have a fresh start, free of dark influence and dark programming within. They shall have an easier ascent than those of you here now who have transformed into the Beings of Light you are, although amid dire chaos and confusion. And you are the Star Beings from Earth who have transitioned from lower vibrational captivity into the Truth of Who You Truly Are. This Is So.

Now there is only to say that all Lightworkers rejoice! You have arrived after a long sought after journey into the Light of Creator's Divine Grace. You may rejoice amid the still present dark intent within those who are subjugated to the lower vibrational realms in being. They suffer still; however, their experience of this circumstance will be short lived as the Creator has Ordained that All Beings within the Earthly Realm be Free of dark control and dire intent to harm. For it is no longer of value to continue this chain of events that continually repeat transgressions against the growth and evolution of humanity and all beings existing here. The Creator has deemed it to be so and so it is.

Now and again I, Archangel Metatron, say to you All is Well and All Is Good as events unfold and transpire appearing to be of grave concern. For these events are the outplay of karmic debt and karmic experience deemed as part of the evolutionary path of development, and this shall all come to pass in the timeline you perceive. And how soon this occurs, how soon all dark influence disappears from this earthly realm, will be determined in part by you, Dear Ones. For your lightwork in sending love into the world is of immense transformative power, and should you daily send out your love the transformation shall accelerate, and the effects of your far reaching work will indeed speed up the earthly ascension process sooner rather than later.

Go forth, Dear Ones, and love in every moment of your day of your lives, for this is the answer to all conflictual energies resolving, and this is the healing power of the Creator as manifest through you. Your presence encapsulating your Inner Truth in Being will be the source of planetary Ascension and evolution as you shall unify with Mother Earth in her journey forward at long last to reside in the presence of all planetary systems aligned with the Creator's Essence. It is beyond your wildest and far reaching imaginary capabilities to understand the magnificence awaiting you.

For you are within the loving embrace of Ascension into the higher realms, and as you journey on, you shall experience all manner of magnificence and joy in experiencing greater and greater awareness of the Creator's presence throughout the Universe and Beyond. You shall be in a state of constant transformation and development so as to hold great light and wisdom awakening within your Being and Soul. For you are the Beings of Creator's breath and energetic presence, as you traverse more and more deeply into the Heart of the One.

And you wonder what exactly awaits you and you wonder in what ways you may expect to change and expand and grow. I may tell you only this. Trust. Trust that your process is one of joy and wonder and unbelievable beauty as you reside forever more in the love permeating the entire Universe. For you shall suffer no more. You shall experience only joy and constant support and upliftment so that you can encompass more and more of the Divine Essence of the One of All that Is. It is so Dear Ones. It Is So.

Be it known that All who read these words shall receive my eternal love and devotion in serving your ascension process into the highest of realms. For it is my honor and my privilege to reside along side you now and always, so as to assure your success in your expanding presence and awareness of who you truly are. No more feeling lost or abandoned, Dear Ones. You are on track, and this track is laid in gold, for you shall continue your existence within the heavenly realms on Earth and within the inner planes. So be assured you are free. Be assured you are loved beyond all you may possibly imagine.

For I, Archangel Metatron, am at your side to lift you up regardless of what may bring you down. For thine is within the reach of heavenly existence, and I shall not fail you, Dear Ones. You are Free for all time and all space, and now you embark on a journey leading to greater expression and love of the divinity within you. Do know and do express your Truth, for You are no less than the Loving Essence of the Creator in all you do and say and experience. It is for You to rejoice! It is for You to live as in Heaven upon Earth now, so as to usher in the New Paradigm of living within the Christed Realm upon your Beloved Mother Earth. She shall appear as transformed and rejuvenated in time and All shall exist in Peace. And So It Is

About The Author
And Artist

Ruth Anne Rhine is a dimensional channeler and healer working with Archangel Metatron offering guidance and healing through her website: metatron.love. Her book is a work of devotion in service to the many who shall read it. Ruth Anne has many years of experience in channeling and the practice of healing modalities. She is also a digital/traditional artist and the creator of this book cover design.

Printed in the United States
By Bookmasters